© Naumann & Göbel Verlagsgesellschaft mbH, a subsidiary of
VEMAG Verlags- und Medien Aktiengesellschaft, Cologne
www.vemag-medien.de

Recipes: Sylvia Winnewisser
Introduction: Doris Ladwig
Design: WirtzCologne

Complete production: Naumann & Göbel Verlagsgesellschaft mbH, Cologne

Printed in Slovenia
07/39
ISBN 978-3-625-01000-5

Swedish Cooking

Contents

Introduction

Endless coasts, impressive mountains, extensive forests — Sweden is a dream destination for many people, with a strikingly varied landscape that entrances every nature lover. And just as rich, clear and unspoiled as the countryside is Swedish cuisine.

Sweden—Lean Harvests and Lavish Tables

With its seemingly infinite forests, wildly foaming rivers and countless crystal clear lakes, sumptuous berry fields and impressive mountain ranges, Sweden is certainly among the most beautiful countries in the world. In surface area, it is about as big as Spain or France and is among the most sparsely populated countries in Europe. Its light settlement has a simple explanation in the harsh northern climate and topographical limitations, which could not produce sufficient food for an expanding population in earlier times. Even a hundred years ago, Sweden was still an impoverished farming country that could barely feed all its citizens. Under these implacable conditions, survival involved backbreaking labor, creativity, and extensive cooperation. Only recently (and aided by technology) has Sweden managed to overcome the severity of its natural setting, and within a single century has transformed itself from a poor agricultural tract into a modern industrial welfare state.

But the older ways of life still shape today's Swedish society: equality and collectivism are strongly entrenched in the Swedish worldview. No one is more valuable than anyone else, and it is assumed and expected that each person will take responsibility for others. Elitism, extravagance, and eccentric lifestyles that stray far from the norm are still inconceivable for many Swedes. Despite their principled way of life, the Swedes have a remarkable ability to celebrate boisterously and enjoy feasts wholeheartedly.

The Swedish soul is fully cognizant of the relationship between the enormity of nature and the smallness of human beings. Solidarity with nature is documented by an ancient traditional law, the *Allemansrätten*, a law that guarantees everyone free access to nature without seeking the landowner's permission. Similarly, berries, mushrooms, and flowers that are not protected under conservation laws may be picked nearly anywhere. Many families take advantage of this right and make annual summer expeditions to collect berries and mushrooms in forests. The best foraging zones, such as *smultronställen*, places where wild strawberries grow, are kept strictly secret, and one generation will pass its knowledge on to the next.

Sweden's pantry

Not surprisingly, with their innumerable lakes and long, winding coasts, the Swedes have a highly developed fishing tradition. Among the freshwater fish, carp, pike, salmon, trout, and char play an important role. Salmon is an especially significant migrant fish. It is pickled, smoked, roasted, poached, or fried and brought to the table for many special holidays, such as Good Friday. *Gravad lax*, known as gravlax, is one specialty that has become internationally famous: pickled and marinated for two to three days, it is then served with a sweet-and-sour mustard sauce.

First among the sea fish is the herring, which has two different designations in Sweden depending on whether or not it originates from the Baltic Sea. If so, it is called *strömming*, and otherwise it is known as *sill*. *Strömming* are smaller and less fatty than *sill*. *Strömming* are known as Baltic herring in English, and a literally breath-taking way of preparing them is described a little further on.

Livestock breeding traditionally focused on cattle and goats, both of which were originally held mainly as sources of dairy products. Meat consumption (which was always meager) was provided for by game: mainly small game such as hare, rabbit, or snow chicken, but also reindeer and moose.

Arable agriculture finds its most favorable conditions in southern Sweden, where the vegetation period amounts to 240 days (the far northern reaches make do with barely half of this period). Grains are the main crops today, planted on about 42 percent of the fields. The usual varieties are barley, wheat, and oats. Flax seed, rape, and (in the extreme south only) sugar beets are also grown. Apart from these, the vegetable garden should not be forgotten, in which relatively cold-resistant cabbage is grown, as well as leguminous plants, notably the yellow pea.

This legume leads directly back to the simple, everyday fare that plays such a significant role in Swedish cooking. By long-established custom, Thursday's menu for many families includes yellow pea soup with pork, which is served with crisp pancakes and berry jam.

Whenever bread-making is mentioned in connection with Sweden, crispbread, or *knäckebröd*, immediately springs to mind. This usually consists of wholegrain wheat, baked very briefly at temperatures around 480 °F/250°C, and after the drying process contains very little water (less than 10 percent). It is typified by its exceptionally long storage life and its flavor only improves the longer it is stored. Unlike the rectangular form common in the rest of Europe, and now in Sweden as well, Swedish crispbread originally resembled an old-fashioned record with a hole in the center (a long-playing record, as the disc is often bigger than a plate). Traditionally, bread was baked in advance for the winter and hung on long poles for storage. Also noteworthy is *tunnbröd*, a thin type of bread. Originally, the dough was pressed flat on a hot stone and cooked on it, but nowadays a non-stick pan makes the work easier. This soft bread is one of the traditional accompaniments of the first *surströmming* of the season (*surströmming* is fermented herring, described on the following page).

Just how much appreciation Swedes have for their berries can be inferred from the old customs concerning the *smultronställen* and other berry-picking spots, mentioned above. The most important berries are strawberries, cloudberries, and lingonberries. The latter, also called cowberries, are hard to find outside Nordic climes, but red currants or, in a pinch, cranberries may be substituted.

No list of common Swedish foods could be considered complete without dill, which is used universally.

As for beverages, especially alcoholic beverages, beer has a major place in Sweden. The country can look back on a brewing tradition that dates from the Middle Ages and the Vikings, who preferred a honey beer, called *mjöd* (similar to mead). In accordance with the country's alcohol regulations, beers are classified by their alcohol content and the strongest are only available in the national liquor stores (*systembolaget*), along with all other spirits.

Regarding stronger liquors, aquavit (*akvavit* in Swedish) is probably the best-known internationally. It is a potent spirit distilled from potatoes or grains and then flavored with caraway, dill, fennel and other aromas. It is consumed well-chilled, sometimes along with beer, and is thought to aid the digestion.

Preservation is everything!

Over the centuries, severe climatic conditions made good house-hold management essential. To survive the long winters, larders were filled with foods such as preserved fish, meat, vegetables, fruit, and bread. The most common procedures for making the foods ready for long storage were drying, salting, and smoking. Thus fishermen dried their catch either by hanging the fish (previously skinned and gutted) on wooden racks or laying them out in the sun on rocky cliffs.

Even today, the first method is still used for cod and its relatives. The result of this air-drying is called stockfish (dried cod). When the dried cod is to be used for a meal at some later time, the fish must first be rehydrated. To this end, it is soaked in water for several days and/or tenderized in a caustic soda solution. During this process, it almost regains its original size. *Lutfisk* with mustard sauce used to be a standard meal served at all celebrations in southern Sweden. Nowadays, it is eaten almost exclusively around Christmastime.

The fish set out to dry on cliffs is called clipfish (salted cod). Unlike the purely air-dried stockfish, clipfish is heavily salted, as well, and is thus "salt-cured" before it dries in the wind. Clipfish was and is still especially prized, above all other preserved fish, in the Nordic countries as well as in Spain, Portugal, Italy, and Brazil.

One very effective method for giving fish and meat long-term durability is putting it into brine and pickling it. However, because the Baltic and North Seas are unsuitable for salt extraction owing to their relatively low salt content, centuries ago salt was a scarce and expensive commodity in the north. Whey (a by-product of cheesemaking) was thus used as an alternative means of preservation.

In northern Sweden, too, the fermentation of lactic acid was exploited for herrings, as it keeps the fish from rotting and needs only a little salt. Headless but with their innards intact, the lightly salted herrings are stored in wooden barrels and then fermented. The highly aromatic *surströmming*, which is eaten from the end of August, is made in this way.

12

Culinary highlights

The smörgåsbord

The *smörgåsbord*, a kind of buffet, has spread the fame of Swedish cuisine far and wide. Following an unwritten rule, it begins with fish dishes. Every conceivable variation of fish is set out on the buffet. This makes the herring the traditional king of the hors d'oeuvre, whether sweet, sour, or salted, as matjes, rollmops, or smoked and marinated in mustard. They may be garnished with onion rings, pickles, red beets, lingonberries, and/or generous quantities of dill, or sauces flavored with curry, garlic or mustard. Various kinds of bread and butter go with this, and a few hot new potatoes boiled in their skins round off the first course.

The second course also consists of cold fish dishes. First and foremost is the salmon, which can be marinated, wood-smoked or cold-smoked, and is often served with a sweet mustard sauce. Sea trout and eel as well as shellfish and crustaceans are also included in this round of dishes.

Next come the meat and poultry dishes. The variety is wide: the spread may include cold pork or roast beef, baked or smoked ham, and roast medallions of lamb, reindeer, moose or other game are served alongside spare ribs, headcheese, pies, and several types of sausage.

There are also small dishes of everyday fare, such as *köttbullar* (meatballs), which are generally accompanied by pickles and lingonberries, or *Janssons frestelse* (Jansson's Temptation), a potato casserole with anchovies, onions, and cream.

This opulent buffet draws to a sweet close with various kinds of cheese followed or accompanied by fruit salads, fresh fruit, puddings, or compotes.

Surströmming

The name *surströmming* is derived from the Swedish *sur* (sour) and *strömming* (Baltic herring) and it is quite a controversial fish delicacy. The new crop of *surströmmingar* are ready for sale annually from mid-August. The fish take half a year to "ripen," and may be recognized by the bloated, almost spherical tins in which they are offered for sale. Here is why the tins swell: in March, the salted and fermented herrings easily fit into their cylindrical tins, where they continue to ferment. The gas pressure resulting from this process is enormous, and its force is exerted in all directions.

On opening (which preferably takes place outdoors), a foul smell escapes from the tin; thus *surströmming* is commonly also called stink fish. It is traditionally consumed with *tunnbröd* topped with almond potatoes, braised onions, and sour cream. The standard accompaniment to the *surströmming* meal is aquavit: one good swig after each bite is the rule.

Sweden celebrates

St. Lucia's Day and Christmas

In the dark period leading up to Christmas, Swedes look forward to the 13th of December. The winter solstice is celebrated throughout the country on St. Lucia's Day.

Wearing floor-length white gowns and decked with crowns of burning candles, light queens are elected in preschools, grade schools, churches, and businesses. The Lucia processions take place in the early morning and are accompanied by attendants, including star boys and children carrying lanterns. The return of the light is announced with solemn singing and the Christmas season is rung in at the same time. In addition to *pepparkakor* (the Swedish form of gingerbread), Swedes traditionally eat *saffransbröd* (a yeast pastry with raisins and saffron) and *lussekatter* (sweet yeast rolls made yellow with saffron and topped with raisins to symbolize Lucia's blinded eyes) on this day. They also drink *glögg*, a Swedish spiced wine that is seasoned with allspice, cinnamon, cardamom, cloves, and ginger and served with raisins and almonds. This beverage accompanies the whole Advent season.

On December 23, Swedes also put up Christmas trees in their homes. Family tradition decides how the tree is decorated. Some adorn it with little blue and yellow Swedish flags, others with tinsel and Christmas ornaments. Christmas Eve is celebrated with relatives and friends, gathering around the tree and exchanging gifts. However, the real highlight of Christmas is the traditional Christmas buffet, the *julbord*, a banquet set out with a wide selection of Swedish specialties. Typical Christmas delicacies include the Christmas ham, pork sausages, *köttbullar* (meatballs), a variety of herring dishes, salads, homemade liver pâté, headcheese, hearty bread, potatoes, and *lutfisk* with peas and sauce. Finally, rice pudding holds an honored place in many families, and is connected with various rituals. For example, an almond may be hidden somewhere in the rice pudding, and superstition has it that whoever finds the almond on their plate will marry during the coming year.

The Swedish Christmas season ends on January 13 with *Tjugondedag Knut*, St. Knut's Day, named after the Swedish king Knut (Canute). This tradition dates back to the end of the eleventh century, and on this day, the Christmas tree is usually dismantled and disposed of.

Easter

It used to be believed in Sweden that between Maundy Thursday and Easter Saturday one might meet up with witches on their way to a celebration with the devil at *Blåkulla*, as their haunt is known in Swedish. Since it is well known that witches travel astride broomsticks, all brooms were hidden in an effort to pre-empt this meeting. Bonfires were also lit to drive off the witches and other evil forces. These days, Easter fires are no longer seen very often, and Easter witches (*påskkärringar*) are met more frequently in the form of disguised children ringing the doorbell to ask for money and sweets.

Foods prepared in honor of Good Friday in Sweden often include either roast lamb or a salmon dish. But Swedish sheep have not yet lambed at that time of year, so the animals slaughtered for the roast are not suckling lambs, but sheep that are as much as a year old.

As a festival, Easter provides yet another opportunity for Swedes to eat well. The Easter buffet, called the *påskbord*, offers a variety of herring, salmon, and egg dishes. *Solöga* (literally "sun's eye") is a must: it consists of a raw egg yolk, topped with an arrangement of anchovies, beets, onions, and capers.

14

Whitsuntide

Even in Sweden, spring finally arrives by Whitsuntide, and nature reappears in a sumptuous green: time for a Swedish spring speciality, *nässelsoppa* (nettle soup). Prepared with freshly picked nettle leaves, it is rich in folic acid, a B-vitamin. Whitsuntide is also the right time to enjoy tender young lamb. The choice of dessert is similarly influenced by seasonal availability: rhubarb compote or rhubarb cakes complete the Whitsun menu.

Midsummer

When the night is nothing more than a few hours of blue dusk in the northernmost reaches of the land, the Swedish festival of festivals is celebrated throughout the country: *midsommar*. On the first weekend after the actual Midsummer's Day (which is June 21), celebrations begin on Friday afternoon and last into the small hours on Saturday. Many places traditionally celebrate with folk music and dances around an enormous pole, called the *majstång* (maypole), which is festively decorated with birch leaves, flowers, garlands, and wreaths. As soon as the pole is raised, there is dancing everywhere: in barns, on commons, and on heaving piers. Good meals and high-proof alcoholic beverages likewise belong to the Midsummer festival, as do old songs (which every Swede can sing by heart, even today). The feast, for which people gather in circles of family and friends as early as the afternoon, consists of herring with dill-spiked potatoes and sour cream.

Kräftskiva: crayfish party

In August's warm dark evenings, traditional crayfish meals help fortify the people in order to face the pain of the passing of the short Swedish summer with courage. Crayfish fests take place throughout the country, providing a chance for dear friends to gather on a veranda lit with Chinese lanterns or in the garden.

Crayfish are sold from the second Thursday of the month, since it is only then that they have reached their full size. These days, however, they no longer come from domestic waters (where they have been virtually wiped out), but are instead imported from Turkey, China, and America. But the Swedes are not to be disuaded, and in any case the crayfish fests are one of their most popular traditions. At *kräftskivor*, people wear little brightly colored paper hats on their heads and celebrate exuberantly in accordance with the motto "a crayfish, a song, and a schnaps."

Hors d'Oeuvres & Snacks

Snacks and hors d'oeuvres made with fish and meat, such as dill herring and chicken salad, enjoy great popularity in Sweden. Experiment with some of the other typically Swedish ways of serving salmon—accompanied by a dill mustard sauce or vinaigrette, or in delicious salmon fishcakes.

Serves 8

2 tomatoes

3 eggs, hard boiled

11 oz/300 g shrimp

1⅔ cups/400 g remoulade

14 oz/400 g
smoked salmon

butter

3 large, round crispbreads
(see p. 136 for recipe)

2 untreated lemons

¼ cucumber

Prep. time: ca. 30 minutes
Per portion ca. 435 kcal/1827 kJ
13 g P, 39 g F, 8 g C

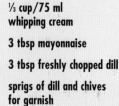

Salmon Stack
Laxtårta med knäckebröd

1 Cut the tomatoes into eighths. Finely chop 1 egg and quarter the rest. Stir half of the shrimp and the chopped egg into about half of the remoulade. Finely chop 5 oz/150 g salmon. Set aside ¼ cup of the remoulade and stir the chopped salmon into the rest.

2 Lightly butter one slice of crispbread. Cover with the salmon filling and set the second crispbread slice on top. Spread the shrimp filling on this and top with the last slice of crispbread. Spread the remaining remoulade over everything.

3 Slice the lemon and cucumber into rounds. Arrange them on top of the stack with the remaining salmon, shrimp, and the egg quarters. Serve with a green salad.

Salmon Cream
Laxkräm

1 Poach the salmon in a little water. Allow to cool, then flake it with a fork and blend with the lemon juice, salt, and paprika.

2 Beat the cream until stiff. Mix the salmon with the mayonnaise, cream and dill. Allow to sit in the refrigerator for at least 1 hour.

3 Spoon the salmon cream onto plates, garnished with sprigs of dill and chives. Accompany simply with hard-boiled eggs, green asparagus or other side dishes to taste.

18

Serves 4

generous 1 lb/500 g
salmon fillet

2½ tbsp lemon juice

1 tsp salt

1 pinch sweet paprika

⅓ cup/75 ml
whipping cream

3 tbsp mayonnaise

3 tbsp freshly chopped dill

sprigs of dill and chives
for garnish

Prep. time: ca. 15 minutes
(plus cooking and cooling time)
Per portion ca. 278 kcal/1165 kJ
24 g P, 20 g F, 2 g C

Långedrag Salad
Långedragssallad

1 Cut the hard stalk from a head of iceberg lettuce and shred the leaves.

2 Trim the leek and slice into rings; trim the peppers and dice or cut them into strips. Toss the vegetables in a salad bowl.

3 Arrange the crayfish at the center of the vegetables with the caviar around them.

4 Boil the eggs for about 10 minutes until hard cooked. Rinse and peel them, then cut into eighths. Arrange the eggs on the vegetables.

5 Season the salad with salt and pepper to taste, garnish with olives and lemon slices, and sprinkle with dill. Accompany simply with salad dressing and fresh bread.

Serves 4

1 head iceberg lettuce

1 leek

1 red pepper

1 green pepper

7 oz/200 g pre-cooked crayfish

1¾ oz/50 g black caviar

1¾ oz/50 g red caviar

2 eggs

salt, pepper

10–20 olives

1 untreated lemon, sliced

dill for garnishing

Prep. time: ca. 30 minutes
Per portion ca. 373 kcal/1565 kJ
23 g P, 27 g F, 10 g C

21

Festive Potatoes with Black Caviar
Festlig potatis med svart kaviar

1 Wash the potatoes thoroughly but do not peel them. Cut into slices approximately ¾ in/2 cm thick. Preheat the oven to 390 °F/200 °C.

2 Grease a metal baking sheet or cover with greaseproof paper and spread the potato pieces over it. Oil lightly and salt.

3 Bake the potatoes in the oven until crisp, about 25 minutes.

4 Wash the cucumber, slice it into disks and cut the disks in half. Arrange the baked potatoes on a large plate and place a half cucumber disk on each. Add a small dab of crème fraîche and 1 tsp of caviar.

5 Slice the lemon into thin circles to garnish the potatoes.

6 Festive Potatoes can be a light lunch or an accompaniment for fish dishes.

Serves 4

4 large potatoes

oil

salt

¼ cucumber

2 tbsp crème fraîche

1¾ oz/50 g black caviar

1 untreated lemon

Prep. time: ca. 30 minutes
(plus cooking time)
Per portion ca. 221 kcal/926 kJ
8 g P, 5 g F, 33 g C

Serves 4

2 salt herrings, pre-cooked

1 bunch dill

1 onion

6 allspice berries

1 cup/250 ml vinegar

4 tbsp sugar

*Prep. time: ca. 20 minutes
(plus time for soaking and
drawing)
Per portion ca. 225 kcal/943 kJ
14 g P, 17 g F, 4 g C*

Dill Herring
Sill i dill

1 Fillet the herrings and soak them in water for at least 12 hours. Then drain and cut the fillets into pieces.

2 Chop the dill finely. Peel the onion and cut into fine rings. Crush the allspice berries in a mortar.

3 In a clay pot, alternate layers of herring, dill, onion, and allspice.

4 Boil the vinegar with 1 cup water, then add the sugar and stir until it dissolves. Pour this mixture over the herrings and allow to draw for at least two days. Accompany Dill Herring simply with boiled potatoes with parsley.

Herring in Tomato Sauce
Sill i tomatsås

1 Fillet the herrings and soak them in water for at least 12 hours. Then cut the fillets into pieces.

2 Place the fish pieces in a dish. Combine the vinegar, oil, tomato purée, sugar, pepper, allspice berries, and 5 tbsp water and pour over the herring pieces. Refrigerate overnight.

3 Chop the chives finely and sprinkle over the herring. Serve with potato salad.

Serves 4

2 salt herrings, pre-cooked

4 tbsp vinegar

3 tbsp oil

6 tbsp tomato purée

4 tsp sugar

pepper

4 allspice berries

½ bunch chives

*Prep. time: ca. 20 minutes
(plus time for soaking and cooling)
Per portion ca. 232 kcal/975 kJ
14 g P, 20 g F, 1 g C*

Salmon with Dill-mustard Sauce
Gravad lax med hovmästarsås

1   Blend the mustard, vinegar, sugar, and seasonings in a bowl.

2   Beat thoroughly until the sugar has completely dissolved.

3   Add the oil one drop at a time, beating vigorously. Finally, stir in the dill and keep the sauce chilled until serving. Serve with the salmon (see recipe opposite).

Salmon with Vinaigrette
Gravad lax med vinaigrette

1   Chop the onion very finely. Finely chop the herbs or blend them in a food processor.

2   Whisk together the vinegar, oil, onion, and herbs and season with salt and pepper.

3   Serve slices of the salmon (see opposite) with vinaigrette.

Salmon with Honey-Dill Sauce
Lax med honungs- och dillsås

1   Finely chop the dill. Whisk the egg yolks well and blend in the sugar, mustard, honey, and cream.

2   Add sufficient lemon juice to give the sauce a sweet-and-sour flavor. Salt and pepper to taste.

3   Stir in the dill and keep the sauce cool until serving. Serve with the salmon (see recipe opposite).

Marinated Salmon (Gravlax)
Gravad lax

1 Finely chop the dill. Combine the salt and sugar in a bowl. Spread half the dill on a large dinner plate. Place one of the two salmon fillets skinside-down on the dill.

2 Take half the sugar and salt mixture and rub well into the salmon. Grind a little pepper, mustard, and allspice over this.

3 Repeat with the other salmon fillet. Then fold up both pieces with the skin on the outside. Cover with foil and chill in the refrigerator for about 3 days.

4 Extract the marinated salmon from its skin and the spices, and cut into very thin slices crosswise. Gravlax is especially good on crispbread, as a snack.

Serves 4

3 bunches dill

4 tbsp salt

5 tbsp sugar

2¼ lb/1 kg salmon, boned and filleted, with skin

1 tbsp peppercorns

mustard seed to taste

allspice to taste

Prep. time: ca. 20 minutes (plus marinating time)
Per portion ca. 278 kcal/1165 kJ
35 g P, 12 g F, 7 g C

25

Swedish Appetizers
Svenska aptitretare

Makes 40 pieces

6 tbsp butter

10 slices rye bread

10 slices white bread

1 iceberg lettuce

10 matjes herring fillets

generous ¾ cup/150 g
diced beets

15 slices reindeer ham

14 oz/400 g
marinated salmon (gravlax)

3 eggs, hard boiled

5 tomatoes

lemon slices

4 tbsp mayonnaise
or remoulade

3 tbsp creamy horseradish

chopped parsley

dill for garnish

Prep. time: ca. 30 minutes
Per piece ca. 68 kcal/285 kJ
5 g P, 4 g F, 3 g C

1 Butter the bread sparingly and cut each slice in half. Cut the hard stalk out of the iceberg lettuce, separate the leaves, and place them on the bread.

2 Cut the matjes herring fillets in half and then cubes, toss with the beets, and spoon over some of the bread slices.

3 Arrange reindeer meat on several slices of bread and the salmon on the remaining pieces.

4 Dice the eggs and tomatoes.

5 Garnish all the open-faced sandwiches as desired with diced egg and tomato, lemon slices, mayonnaise or remoulade, creamy horseradish, and herbs. A cold beer goes well with this!

26

Caviar on Toast
Kaviar på toast

Serves 4

4 slices rye bread

5 tbsp butter

7 oz/200 g
North Sea shrimp

8 tbsp mayonnaise

1 tbsp tomato purée

1 splash
Worcestershire sauce

½ lemon

7 oz/200 g lumpfish roe

freshly chopped dill
to garnish

Prep. time: ca. 15 minutes
(plus roasting time)
Per portion ca. 453 kcal/1900 kJ
24 g P, 30 g F, 17 g C

1 Cut out circles of bread with a glass or biscuit cutter. Warm the butter in a pan and fry the bread circles in it. Allow to cool.

2 Combine the shrimp with the mayonnaise, tomato purée, and Worcestershire sauce. Place the mixture on the fried bread circles.

3 Peel the lemon, remove the skin, and cut into small pieces. Serve each bread circle garnished with lemon and fresh dill.

Crab Salad
Krabbsallad

1 Shred the lettuce into fine strips. Peel the shallots and chop them finely. Trim and dice the pepper and celery. Peel and crush the garlic.

2 Heat the oil in a pan. Lightly brown the shallots, pepper, celery and garlic, and simmer gently for about 10 minutes.

3 Allow the vegetable mixture to cool, then combine with mustard, mayonnaise and Worcestershire sauce. Salt and pepper to taste.

4 Stir the crabmeat into the vegetable dressing. Arrange shreds of lettuce on plates and distribute the crab salad on top. Serve sprinkled with parsley. Rye bread is good with this dish.

Serves 4

1 head of lettuce

4 shallots

1 green pepper

½ celeriac

1 garlic clove

2 tbsp oil

1 tbsp mild mustard

generous ⅔ cup/180 g mayonnaise

1 splash Worcestershire sauce

salt, pepper

1 lb/450 g crabmeat, pre-cooked

2 tbsp chopped fresh parsley

Prep. time: ca. 35 minutes
Per portion ca. 485 kcal/2037 kJ
23 g P, 41 g F, 6 g C

29

West Coast Salad
Västkustsallad

1 Tip the crabmeat and mussels in a sieve to drain. Thaw and heat the peas in a little salted water. Peel the asparagus and cook it to al dente in a little butter (for approximately 15 minutes).

2 Trim the mushrooms and slice them finely. Cut the cooled asparagus into pieces. Drain the corn. Tear the lettuce leaves into bite-sized pieces.

3 For the salad dressing, blend the vinegar and oil, and add salt and pepper to taste.

4 Toss everthing in a salad bowl and pour the dressing over it. Serve garnished with fresh dill. Offer Swedish unleavened bread on the side.

Serves 4

7 oz/200 g crabmeat (fresh or from a jar)

5 oz/150 g mussels (fresh or from a jar)

1 cup/150 g frozen peas

¾ lb/350 g tender asparagus

½ tsp butter

5 oz/150 g mushrooms

½ cup/75 g corn

½ head iceberg lettuce

4 tbsp red wine vinegar

6 tbsp sunflower oil

salt, pepper

dill for garnish

Prep. time: ca. 45 minutes
Per portion ca. 323 kcal/1355 kJ
20 g P, 17 g F, 22 g C

30

Serves 4

1 small soup chicken

7 oz/200 g mushrooms

1 red pepper

1 bunch celery

1 chicory

3 tbsp vinegar

4 tbsp sunflower oil

4 tbsp chicken stock

½ tsp mustard

salt, pepper

powdered paprika

Prep. time: ca. 20 minutes
(plus cooking and cooling time)
Per portion ca. 123 kcal/515 kJ
10 g P, 8 g F, 3 g C

Chicken Salad
Kycklingsallad

1 Boil the chicken gently for approximately 60 minutes, depending on its size. Cool, then remove the skin and the meat from the bones, then cut the meat into small pieces.

2 Trim and slice the mushrooms. Trim and dice the pepper and celery. Cut the chicory into fine strips.

3 Combine the chicken meat and vegetables in a bowl.

4 Prepare a salad dressing with the vinegar, oil, chicken stock, and mustard. Blend well. Add salt, pepper, and paprika to taste, and toss with the salad.

5 Allow the salad to rest in the refrigerator for at least 30 minutes before serving.

Game Salad with Lingonberries
Viltsallad med lingon

1 Combine the lingonberries (or red currants), red wine, orange peel, and sugar in a pot. Bring to a boil, then allow to cool.

2 Rub salt and pepper into the venison steaks. Trim and halve the chanterelles. Heat 3 tbsp of the oil in a pan and sear the steaks about 4 minutes on each side. Remove from the pan and wrap in aluminum foil to keep warm.

3 Brown the chanterelles in the same pan in 1 tbsp oil. Peel, core, and slice the pears. Add to the pan and sear in 1 tbsp oil.

4 Strain the lingonberries from their cooking liquid (retain both). Use the remaining oil to prepare a salad dressing with the vinegar, lingonberry cooking juices, salt and pepper. Place the lollo rosso leaves on four plates. Slice the steaks into fine medallions.

5 Arrange the medallions on the lettuce leaves. Top with the chanterelles, pears, and lingonberries, and sprinkle with the salad dressing. Accompany with roasted potatoes.

Serves 4

1½ cups/150 g lingonberries

7 tbsp/100 ml red wine

peel of ½ untreated orange

1 tbsp sugar

salt, pepper

11 oz/300 g venison steak

5 oz/150 g chanterelles

9 tbsp oil

2 pears

3 tbsp red wine vinegar

½ head lollo rosso

Prep. time: ca. 30 minutes (plus browning time)
Per portion ca. 216 kcal/905 kJ
19 g P, 6 g F, 18 g C

Serves 4

⅔ cup/150 g sugar

1 tsp pink peppercorns

1 tsp white peppercorns

2 bay leaves

juice of 2 lemons

6–8 matjes herring fillets, soaked in water

1 onion

1 leek

1 bunch freshly chopped dill

*Prep. time: ca. 30 minutes
(plus marinating time)
Per portion ca. 383 kcal/1607 kJ
15 g P, 17 g F, 41 g C*

Serves 4

6–8 matjes herring fillets, soaked in water

5 shallots

15 stuffed olives

1 cup/250 g ketchup

4 tbsp vinegar

4 tbsp sugar

1 tsp salt

1 tsp white pepper

5 tbsp oil

*Prep. time: ca. 20 minutes
(plus marinating time)
Per portion ca. 403 kcal/1690 kJ
16 g P, 29 g F, 20 g C*

Serves 4

1¼ cups/300 ml vinegar

7 tbsp/100 g sugar

½ tbsp white peppercorns

¼ tsp anise

¼ tsp caraway seeds

3 cloves, 3 juniper berries

2 red onions

6–8 matjes herring fillets, soaked in water

3 tbsp aquavit

1 tsp lemon zest

*Prep. time: ca. 15 minutes
(plus marinating time)
Per portion ca. 320 kcal/1344 kJ
14 g P, 17 g F, 27 g C*

Sweet-&-Sour Pickled Herrings
Inlagd sötsur sill

1 In a saucepan, boil the sugar and spices with the lemon juice and ⅔ cup/150 ml water to make a sauce. Allow to cool.

2 Drain the matjes herring fillets well and cut into pieces. Peel and chop the onion, and trim the leek and slice it into thin rings.

3 Distribute the onion, leek, herring pieces, and dill in a serving dish in alternating layers. Strain the sauce carefully and pour over everything. Marinate overnight before serving.

Pickled Herrings with Tomatoes
Inlagd sill med tomater

1 Drain the herrings and cut them into small pieces. Peel and slice the shallots into rings.

2 Place the herring pieces, shallots, and olives in a dish.

3 Mix together the ketchup, vinegar, sugar, salt, and pepper. Slowly pour in the oil and blend well.

4 Pour this marinade over the herrings and allow to draw in the refrigerator for several hours.

Pickled Herrings with Aquavit
Inlagd sill med akvavit

1 Make a sauce by heating the vinegar, sugar, and spices, then let it cool.

2 Peel and slice the onions into thin rings. Drain the herrings and cut them into pieces.

3 Alternate layers of herring and onion in a serving dish. Boil the sauce with the aquavit and lemon zest, then pour it over the herrings. Refrigerate for several hours.

Glaziers' Herrings
Glasmästarsill

1 Fillet the herrings (retain the spine) and let them soak in water overnight. The next day, rinse and cut into pieces about ¾ in/2 cm thick.

2 Bring the vinegar and to a boil in a small pan. Stir gently until the sugar has dissolved. Allow the sauce to cool.

3 Peel the onions and carrots. Slice both thinly. Peel and finely grate the horseradish and ginger.

4 Layer everything alternately in a serving dish. Cover with a layer of the spices and bay leaves. Finally, pour the cooled sauce over the top and set aside. Refrigerate for several days. Glaziers' Herrings taste best with bread or potato salad.

Serves 4

4 fresh matjes

2 cups/500 ml vinegar

⅔ cup/150 g sugar

2 red onions, 2 carrots

1 oz/25 g horseradish

½ oz/15 g fresh ginger root

1½ tsp allspice berries

2 tsp mustard seed

3 bay leaves

Prep. time: ca. 50 minutes (plus time for soaking and marinating)
Per portion ca. 448 kcal/1879 kJ
22 g P, 26 g F, 31 g C

Stuffed Eggs
Fyllda ägg

Serves 4

4–6 eggs

3½ oz/100 g cream cheese

2 tbsp cream

½ tsp crushed green peppercorns

sweet paprika

grated zest of 1 untreated lemon

2 slices smoked ham

½ bunch freshly chopped parsley

Prep. time: ca. 20 minutes (plus cooking time)
Per portion ca. 206 kcal/863 kJ
13 g P, 16 g F, 2 g C

1 Hard boil the eggs (approximately 10 minutes) and allow them to cool. Peel, cut in half horizontally and reserve each top white half.

2 Carefully spoon out the egg yolks and press through a sieve. Combine the yolk with the cream cheese and cream. Chop the reserved egg whites and add to the egg mixture, along with the green pepper, paprika, and lemon zest.

3 Put the egg mixture into a large icing bag and squeeze into each egg half. Place the ham strips in small cups and set the eggs on top, garnished with parsley. Accompany with plain white bread.

Meat-filled Roll-ups
Tunnbrödsrullar fyllda med lax eller renkött

Serves 4

¼ head lettuce

4 tbsp sweet mustard

2 tbsp honey

4 tbsp freshly chopped dill

salt

pepper

4 pieces Swedish *tunnbröd* (soft, thin bread or sandwich wraps)

3 tbsp butter

2 tbsp creamy horseradish (from the jar, or mix whipped cream and grated horseradish)

3½ oz/100 g smoked reindeer meat

7 oz/200 g marinated salmon (gravlax)

Prep. time: ca. 15 minutes
Per portion ca. 130 kcal/543 kJ
15 g P, 6 g F, 5 g C

1 Shred the lettuce finely. Thoroughly combine the mustard, honey, and dill. Season to taste with salt and pepper.

2 Butter the *tunnbröd*. Top two pieces of bread with some of the shredded lettuce.

3 Top those two breads with reindeer meat and some horseradish cream.

4 Coat the other two slices of bread with the honey-mustard sauce and top with the salmon.

5 Roll up each bread and cut into ¾ in/2 cm pieces.

Stuffed Bread
Bröd med fyllning

1 Preheat the oven to 465 °F/240 °C. Cut several pockets into the top of the loaf.

2 Lay out aluminum foil on a work surface. Set the bread on it. Peel and chop the onion.

3 Chop the sausage, cheese, and tomatoes and combine with the onion. Fold in the butter and parsley.

4 Heap this mixture into the bread pockets. Seal the loaf in the kitchen foil and bake in the oven for about 15 minutes. Cucumber salad goes well with this.

Serves 4

1 white or rye bread

1 onion

3½ oz/100 g smoked sausage

3½ oz/100 g cheese

2 tomatoes

5 tbsp butter, flaked

freshly chopped parsley

Prep. time: ca. 35 minutes
Per portion ca. 249 kcal/1046 kJ
12 g P, 20 g F, 6 g C

37

Swedish Hot Dogs
Svensk varmkorv

1 Bring a generous quantity of water to a boil, then reduce the heat. Warm the hot dogs in the hot, but not boiling, water. Avoid bursting the skins. Preheat the oven to 390 °F/200 °C.

2 Slice the pickles into thin rings. Warm the hot dog buns in the oven for about 10 minutes. Then cut them almost through lengthwise, leaving the two halves attached.

3 Place the warm hot dogs inside the buns and add ketchup, mayonnaise, and mustard.

4 Add the sliced pickles to the buns and top off with the crispy fried onions.

Serves 4

4 hot dogs

2 large pickles

4 hot dog buns

4 tbsp curry ketchup

4 tsp mayonnaise

1 tsp Swedish mustard

4 tbsp dried fried onions

Prep. time: ca. 30 minutes
Per portion ca. 280 kcal/1176 kJ
9 g P, 15 g F, 26 g C

Makes 8

8 vol-au-vent cases

1–1¾ lb/500–750 g cod fillets

lemon juice; salt

1 cup/250 ml fish stock

½ cup/125 ml dry white wine

3½ oz/100 g mushrooms

2½ tbsp/40 g butter

generous 1 lb/500 g mussels

1 tbsp flour

3½ oz/100 g crab meat

pepper; 1 egg yolk

3 tbsp cream

*Prep. time: ca. 30 minutes
(plus cooking and simmering time)
Per piece ca. 277 kcal/1165 kJ
22 g P, 15 g F, 10 g C*

Fish Vol-au-Vents
Krustad med fisk

1   Clean the fish fillets. Sprinkle with the lemon juice and salt.

2   Bring the fish stock to a boil, add the white wine, and cook the fish fillets in it for about 8 minutes.

3   Trim and slice the mushrooms, and sauté in a little butter. Clean the mussels carefully, boil in salted water, and remove from their shells.

4   Heat the mussels in butter, dust with the flour, and add to the fish stock. Allow to simmer for about 10–12 minutes.

5   Drain the mussels from the stock and chop coarsely. Combine with the crab meat, add salt and pepper to taste, and blend with the egg yolk and cream.

6   Bake the vol-au-vent cases in the oven according to the instructions on the package. Fill with the fish mixture and serve.

Fish Terrine
Fiskterrin

1   Purée the pike fillet in a food processor, then press it through a sieve. Stir in the cream and season with salt, pepper, and nutmeg. Refrigerate or place the mixture over a dish of ice cubes.

2   Slice the salmon fillet into wide strips and season with salt and pepper. Chill in the refrigerator.

3   Blanch the spinach leaves briefly, then refresh in cold water and allow to cool. Lay out some plastic wrap. Spread the spinach leaves on it, topped by the salmon strips. Roll up the salmon carefully with the help of the plastic wrap.

4   Preheat the oven to 300 °F/150 °C. Fill a frying pan with about 2 in/5 cm water.

5   Fill a greased pâté dish (2 cups/.5 liter) with half of the pike mousse. Add the roll of salmon in spinach (without the plastic wrap) and top with the remaining pike mousse. Cover with aluminum foil and cook in a water bath for about 90 minutes.

6   Serve the terrine thoroughly chilled.

Serves 8

generous 1 lb/500 g pike fillet

⅔ cup/150 ml heavy cream

salt, freshly ground white pepper

1 pinch freshly grated nutmeg

generous 1 lb/500 g fresh salmon fillet

12 large spinach leaves

Prep. time: ca. 20 minutes (plus cooking and chilling time)
Per portion ca. 288 kcal/1208 kJ 27 g P, 19 g F, 2 g C

Soups

A soup warms the stomach and whets the appetite for the foods to follow. In this chapter, cherished traditional Swedish dishes await discovery. Get ready to enjoy Yellow Pea Soup, Crab Soup, spring-fresh Nettle Soup, and many more.

Carrot Soup
Morotssoppa

Serves 4

14 oz/400 g carrots

2 onions, 2 apples

1 tbsp butter

½ tsp fresh ginger

½ tsp ground cinnamon

2 cups/500 ml vegetable stock

⅔ cup/150 ml orange juice

salt, pepper

10 tbsp/150 g crème fraîche

4 elderflowers

oil for frying

Prep. time: ca. 20 minutes (plus cooking time)
Per portion ca. 208 kcal/873 kJ
3 g P, 14 g F, 17 g C

1 Peel and finely chop the carrots. Peel and dice the onions. Peel, core, and dice the apples.

2 Heat the butter in a large pot and sauté the onions in it. Add the carrots and apples. Grate the ginger and add it with the cinnamon. Cook everything together briefly.

3 Pour in the stock and orange juice and simmer for about 15 minutes. Purée the soup and add salt and pepper to taste. Stir in the crème fraîche.

4 Wash and drain the elderflowers, then fry in hot oil until crisp and add to the soup. Serve with white bread.

Nettle Soup
Nässelsoppa

Serves 4

2¼ lb/1 kg young nettles

2 tbsp butter

1 qt/1 liter chicken stock

3 tbsp cornflour

salt

pepper

4 tbsp crème fraîche

Prep. time: ca. 45 minutes
Per portion ca. 152 kcal/638 kJ
14 g P, 3 g F, 16 g C

1 Strip the nettle leaves from the stalks and wash (do not dry).

2 Heat the butter in a large pot, add the wet nettle leaves and steam them, stirring, until they wilt.

3 Pour in the stock and simmer for about 15 minutes, then purée. Bring the soup to a boil.

4 Dissolve the cornflour in 1 tbsp water and use it to thicken the soup. Season to taste with salt and pepper. Stir in the crème fraîche. Serve with toasted whole-wheat rolls.

Forest Mushroom Soup
Soppa på blandsvamp

1 Trim the mushrooms and slice thinly. Peel the onion and garlic and chop thoroughly.

2 Heat the butter in a deep pot and brown the mushrooms, onions, and garlic for about 5 minutes.

3 Sprinkle the mushrooms with the flour and pour in the stock. Blend well and simmer for several minutes until the soup thickens.

4 Season the mushroom soup with cream, sherry, and salt and pepper to taste. Distribute into bowls and serve garnished with the parsley. Accompany with cheese straws.

Serves 4

14 oz/400 g mixed forest mushrooms, fresh or canned

1 onion

1 clove garlic

2 tbsp butter

3 tbsp flour

3⅓ cups/800 ml vegetable stock

7 tbsp/100 ml cream

2 tbsp sherry

salt, pepper

2 tbsp chopped fresh parsley

Prep. time: ca. 30 minutes (plus browning time)
Per portion ca. 147 kcal/616 kJ
4 g P, 12 g F, 5 g C

Chilled Cucumber Soup
Kall gurksoppa

1 Peel and halve the cucumber and remove the seeds with a spoon. Chop up the cucumber, then purée it in a blender. Peel and crush the garlic.

2 Combine the puréed cucumber with the garlic, filmjolk or crème fraîche, cream, and lemon juice. Season with salt and pepper to taste. Transfer to a bowl and chill.

3 Chop the dill well and stir up to 2 tbsp into the soup, then chill until ready to serve.

4 Fill soup bowls with the well-chilled soup and serve garnished with the crayfish meat and dill. Toasted whole-wheat rolls make a good accompaniment.

Serves 4

1 large cucumber

1 clove garlic

generous ¾ cup/200 ml filmjolk (Swedish dairy product) or crème fraîche

⅔ cup/150 ml cream

2 tbsp lemon juice

salt, pepper

1 bunch dill

3½ oz/100 g pre-cooked crayfish meat

Prep. time: ca. 20 minutes (plus chilling time)
Per portion ca. 174 kcal/731 kJ
8 g P, 13 g F, 6 g C

Serves 4

1 large crab, boiled

3 tbsp butter

1 onion

2 tbsp flour

4¼ cups/1.15 liters milk

6 tbsp/90 ml sherry

salt, pepper, nutmeg

⅔ cup/150 ml
heavy cream

½ bunch fresh chives,
chopped finely

*Prep. time: ca. 30 minutes
(plus cooking time)
Per portion ca. 338 kcal/1418 kJ
6 g P, 17 g F, 6 g C*

Crab Soup
Fin kräftsoppa

1 Shell the crab. Then cut open the legs and claws and scoop out the flesh.

2 Transfer the crab to a bowl and remove the giblets. Press out the stomach and remove it. Scoop out the white meat and set it aside. Scoop out the dark crabmeat.

3 Heat the butter in a deep pot. Peel the onion, chop finely and cook in the butter until transparent. Dust with the flour and pour in the milk and sherry. Stir thoroughly and boil until the mixture thickens.

4 Add the dark crabmeat to the soup and simmer for 20 minutes. Season with salt, pepper, and nutmeg to taste. Then stir in the white crabmeat and the clawmeat and simmer for an additional 5 minutes.

5 Distribute the crab soup into bowls. Beat the cream until stiff and float a dollop on each bowl. Garnish with chives and serve with toasted whole-wheat rolls.

Creamy Fish Soup
Krämig fisksoppa

1 Cut the fish fillets into small pieces. Peel and finely dice the onion and garlic. Peel the potatoes and slice into thin rounds.

2 Heat the butter in a deep pot and sauté the onions and garlic. Add the potatoes and briefly fry them. Pour in 7 tbsp/ 100 ml water and simmer for about 10 minutes.

3 Add the tomatoes, parsley, bay leaves, and spices, followed by the fish pieces. Pour in the fish stock and simmer for a further 8 minutes.

4 Stir the cream into the soup and season to taste. Remove the bay leaves and garnish the soup with fresh dill. Accompany with toast.

Serves 4

14 oz/400 g white fish fillets

1 onion, 2 cloves garlic

4 potatoes

3 tbsp butter

14 oz/400 g tomatoes (canned)

½ bunch fresh parsley, chopped

2 bay leaves

salt, pepper

1 pinch cayenne pepper

2 cups/500 ml fish stock

7 tbsp/100 ml cream

dill for garnish

Prep. time: ca. 20 minutes (plus cooking time)
Per portion ca. 209 kcal/878 kJ 19 g P, 13 g F, 5 g C

Yellow Pea Soup with Vegetables
Gul ärtsoppa med grönsaker

Serves 4

2 cups/400 g dried yellow peas

2 carrots, 2 onions

7 oz/200 g celeriac

1 leek

7 oz/200 g smoked bacon

3⅓ cups/800 ml vegetable stock

salt, pepper

1 pinch coriander

½ bunch cilantro, chopped

Prep. time: ca. 30 minutes (plus cooking time)
Per portion ca. 410 kcal/1722 kJ 35 g P, 7 g F, 49 g C

1 Prepare pea soup as described in steps 1 and 2, opposite.

2 Peel the carrots, onions, and celeriac. Trim the leek, and chop all the vegetables into small pieces. Finely dice the bacon.

3 Sweat the diced bacon in a deep pot, then remove and set aside. Sweat the vegetables gently in the bacon fat.

4 Add the yellow peas and vegetable stock to the cooking juices. Simmer for 1 hour 30 minutes. Purée the soup, then add salt, pepper, and coriander to taste. Garnish with bacon and cilantro.

Yellow Pea Soup with Sausage
Gul ärtsoppa med wienerkorv

Serves 4

2 cups/400 g dried yellow peas

1 onion

1 tbsp oil

3⅓ cups/800 ml vegetable stock

salt, pepper

7 tbsp/100 ml cream

4 Vienna sausages

½ bunch fresh parsley, chopped

Prep. time: ca. 15 minutes (plus cooking time)
Per portion ca. 603 kcal/2530 kJ 35 g P, 31 g F, 45 g C

1 Prepare pea soup as described in steps 1 and 2, opposite.

2 Peel and chop the onion. Heat the oil in a deep pot and fry the onion gently. Add the peas and vegetable stock to this and cook together for about 1 hour 30 minutes.

3 Purée the soup, then add salt and pepper to taste and stir in the cream. Slice the Vienna sausages and warm through in the soup. Serve garnished with the parsley.

Yellow Pea Soup with Chicken
Gul ärtsoppa med stekt hönsbröst

Serves 4

2 cups/400 g dried yellow peas

1 onion

3 tbsp oil

3⅓ cups/800 ml chicken stock

12 oz/350 g chicken breast fillet

salt, pepper

curry powder

Prep. time: ca. 20 minutes (plus cooking time)
Per portion ca. 432 kcal/1817 kJ 49 g P, 5 g F, 47 g C

1 Prepare pea soup as described in steps 1 and 2, opposite.

2 Peel and chop the onion, and sauté lightly in 1 tbsp hot oil. Add the peas and chicken stock to the pan and simmer for about 1 hour 30 minutes.

3 Just before the end of the cooking time, heat the remaining oil and brown the chicken breast fillet on both sides until it is crisp. Remove from the pan, season and cut into strips.

4 Purée the pea soup, add curry powder to taste, and serve with the chicken strips.

Yellow Pea Soup with Pork
Gul ärtsoppa med rimmat fläsk

1 Rinse and sort the dried peas and soak them overnight in plenty of water. Drain.

2 Bring the peas to a boil in 1½ quarts/1.5 liters fresh water, skimming away any floating skins from time to time. Boil for about 20 minutes, then set aside.

3 Peel and chop the onions. Heat the butter in a large pot and sweat the onions. Add the pork and cook with the onions briefly. Pour in the peas with their cooking water, and add the beef stock.

4 Simmer the soup for about 1 hour 10 minutes. Remove the meat, slice or dice it, and return it to the soup. Season with salt, pepper and marjoram. Serve with brown mustard and fresh bread as desired.

Serves 4

2 cups/400 g dried yellow peas

2 onions

1 tbsp butter

13 oz/375 g cured pork

3⅓ cups/800 ml beef stock

salt, pepper

1 tsp marjoram

*Prep. time: ca. 20 minutes (plus soaking and cooking time)
Per portion ca. 473 kcal/1985 kJ
46 g P, 11 g F, 45 g C*

49

Saint Germain Pea Soup
Grön ärtsoppa Saint-Germain

Serves 4

1 large onion

3 tbsp butter

1 qt/1 liter veal stock

2 cups/300 g peas

1 tbsp flour

2 tbsp sherry

1 egg yolk

7 tbsp/100 ml cream

salt, pepper

freshly grated horseradish,
croutons for garnish

Prep. time: ca. 20 minutes
(plus cooking time)
Per portion ca. 328 kcal/1376 kJ
8 g P, 27 g F, 13 g C

1   Peel and dice the onion. Heat 1 tbsp of the butter in a deep pan and sauté the onion until transparent. Pour in the veal stock and add the peas. Bring to a boil and simmer for about 20 minutes, then purée the soup.

2   Heat the remaining butter in a soup pot and brown the flour. While stirring continuously, incorporate the soup and then add the sherry.

3   Mix the egg yolk with the cream and stir vigorously into the soup. Season to taste with salt and pepper, and serve with horseradish and cheese croutons.

Blood Soup
Svartsoppa

Serves 4

2 qts/2 liters beef stock

3 tbsp flour

1⅔ cups/400 ml
pig or goose blood

1 tbsp salt

1 tbsp sugar

1 tsp finely grated ginger

1 tsp ground clove

generous ¾ cup/200 g
thick fruit jelly (plum, currant, etc.)

2 tbsp white vinegar

3 tbsp aquavit

7 tbsp/100 ml sherry

Prep. time: ca. 20 minutes
(plus cooking time)
Per portion ca. 100 kcal/418 kJ
10 g P, 1 g F, 11 g C

1   Pour the stock in a deep pot and bring to a boil. Combine the flour and blood and add a little of the hot stock, beating well.

2   Add the blood mixture to the boiling stock and whisk vigorously to prevent clumps forming. Simmer the soup for about 10 minutes, stirring constantly.

3   Add the salt, sugar, and remaining spices to the soup, along with the fruit jelly, vinegar, aquavit, and sherry. Traditional accompaniments are goose giblets or liver sausage.

Vegetable Soup with Shrimp
Grönsakssoppa med räkor

1   Trim, peel, and dice the carrots, potatoes, and kohlrabi. Cull, trim, and thoroughly wash the spinach.

2   Heat the stock in a large pot. Add the carrots, potatoes, kohlrabi, and peas. Simmer for about 15 minutes. Meanwhile, chop the parsley finely.

3   Add the spinach to the soup and simmer for 5 minutes longer. Whisk together the egg yolk and cream, and stir into the soup. Season with salt and pepper.

4   Finally, add the parsley and crabmeat to the soup and heat through briefly. Serve garnished with dill. Accompany with a baguette.

Serves 4

7 oz/200 g carrots

7 oz/200 g potatoes

9 oz/250 g kohlrabi

5 oz/150 g spinach leaves

⅔ cup/100 g peas

1 qt/1 liter vegetable stock

½ bunch parsley

1 egg yolk

7 tbsp/100 ml cream

salt, pepper

5 oz/150 g North Sea shrimp, pre-cooked

dill for garnish

*Prep. time: ca. 30 minutes
(plus cooking time)
Per portion ca. 228 kcal/956 kJ
15 g P, 10 g F, 18 g C*

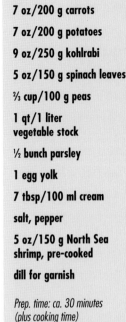

53

Green Cabbage Soup with Bologna
Grönkålssoppa med fläskkorv

1   Wash and trim the cabbage and cut out the hard stalk. Separate the cabbage leaves and cut off any brittle parts.

2   Bring 2 quarts/2 liters water to a boil in a large pot. Add the green cabbage leaves and blanch for about 10 minutes.

3   Remove the cabbage leaves from the water with a skimmer and drain. Chop them finely or blend in a food processor.

4   Heat the butter in a pot and sprinkle on the flour. Brown briefly, then pour in the stock while stirring continuously. Continue to cook and allow to thicken.

5   Add the green cabbage to the soup and bring to a boil. Simmer for 5 minutes. Season with salt, pepper, the nutmeg, and the cream.

6   Slice or dice the bologna and serve in the soup or as a separate accompaniment.

Serves 4

generous 1 lb/500 g green cabbage

2 tbsp butter

3 tbsp flour

1 qt/1 liter vegetable stock

salt, pepper

½ tsp finely grated nutmeg

7 tbsp/100 ml cream

14 oz/400 g bologna

*Prep. time: ca. 20 minutes
(plus cooking time)
Per portion ca. 423 kcal/1775 kJ
19 g P, 37 g F, 4 g C*

Serves 4

14 oz/400 g potatoes

1 leek, 1 onion

4 tbsp butter

salt, pepper

whole nutmeg

1 tsp mustard

zest and juice of ½ untreated lemon

2 cups/500 ml fish stock

½ cup/125 ml cream

generous 1 lb/500 g cod fillet

1 egg yolk

2 tbsp chopped fresh herbs (chives, parsley, dill, chervil)

Prep. time: ca. 30 minutes (plus cooking time)
Per portion ca. 303 kcal/1271 kJ
28 g P, 13 g F, 18 g C

Fish Stew with Herbs
Fiskgryta med kryddörter

1 Peel and dice the potatoes. Trim the leek, removing the dark green parts. Wash the remaining leek thoroughly and slice into rings. Peel and dice the onion.

2 Melt the butter in a deep pot and sauté the diced onion until transparent. Add the potatoes and leek and cook gently. Season with salt, pepper, freshly grated nutmeg, mustard, and lemon zest.

3 Pour in the fish stock and gently stir in 7 tbsp/100 ml of the cream. Bring to a boil and then simmer over low heat for 15–20 minutes.

4 Wash the fish fillets, pat dry, and cut into cubes. Sprinkle with the lemon juice and rub with salt and pepper.

5 Combine the diced fish with the vegetables and cook for a further 10 minutes.

6 Whisk the egg yolk with the remaining cream and stir into the soup. Do not let the soup boil again. Sprinkle the fresh herbs over the fish stew and serve.

Cream of Mussel Soup
Krämig musselsoppa

1 Trim the mussels carefully and debeard. Discard any open mussels. Trim the soup vegetables and chop into small pieces. Peel and coarsely chop the garlic clove.

2 Heat the oil in a deep pot and sauté the vegetables and garlic in it. Then pour in the wine and add the mussels. Simmer for about 15 minutes.

3 Remove the mussels from the pot and reserve the cooking liquid. Discard any closed mussels. Extract the mussel flesh from the open shells and reserve in a bowl.

4 Dice the bacon and render it in a soup pot, then remove the bacon. Peel and dice the onions and fry in the bacon fat.

5 Peel and dice the potatoes. Dust the onions with the flour. Add the potatoes, milk, and mussel-cooking liquid to the pan and season with salt and pepper. Cover and simmer for 10 minutes.

6 Finally, stir in the cream, bacon, and mussels and simmer for 3 more minutes.

Serves 4

2¾ lb/1.25 kg mussels

1 bunch soup vegetables

1 clove garlic

1 tbsp oil

3¼ cups/750 ml dry white wine

3½ oz/100 g smoked bacon

2 onions

3 potatoes

1 tbsp flour

1 cup/250 ml milk

salt, pepper

1 cup/250 ml cream

*Prep. time: ca. 45 minutes
(plus cooking time)
Per portion ca. 540 kcal/2268 kJ
41 g P, 29 g F, 26 g C*

Vegetables & Side Dishes

The traditional side for Swedish meals is the versatile potato, which arrives on the table in numerous delicious variations, whether as a salad or a dumpling, or in its best-known and most delectable form as the baked dish aptly named "Jansson's Temptation." Cabbage and root vegetables are also on the menu. Some of these sides are hearty enough to make a meal in themselves!

Serves 4

1 small white cabbage

1 leek

4 carrots

6 pickles

7 tbsp/100 ml oil

**7 tbsp/100 ml
apple cider vinegar**

2 tbsp sugar

1 tsp salt

1½ tsp black pepper

½ bunch parsley

*Prep. time: ca. 25 minutes
Per portion ca. 163 kcal/687 kJ
3 g P, 13 g F, 7 g C*

Coleslaw with Cucumbers
Vitkålssallad med gurka

1 Trim the cabbage, pull the leaves from the stalk, wash them and remove any brittle parts. Thinly slice the leaves.

2 Trim the leek and remove the green part. Wash the rest well and slice into fine rings. Peel and finely grate the carrots. Chop the pickles. Mix the vegetables together.

3 For the dressing, combine the oil, vinegar, sugar, salt, and black pepper in a small saucepan and bring to a boil. Pour over the vegetables while still hot.

4 Chop the parsley and sprinkle over the salad.

Serves 4

generous 1 lb/500 g beets

1 apple

**1 small piece horseradish
(approx. ⅓ in/1 cm)**

2 tbsp lemon juice

**generous ¾ cup/200 g
sour cream**

salt

pepper

*Prep. time: ca. 20 minutes
(plus cooking and drawing time)
Per portion ca. 119 kcal/498 kJ
4 g P, 5 g F, 14 g C*

Beet Salad
Rödbetssallad

1 Scrub and rinse the beets well. Boil them in their peel for approximately 30 minutes. Drain and cool.

2 Peel the beets and cut into fine strips. Peel, core, and dice the apple. Peel the horseradish root and grate it finely. Combine these ingredients in a bowl.

3 Whisk together the lemon juice, sour cream, horseradish, salt, and pepper into a salad dressing.

4 Pour the salad dressing over the beets and allow to draw for at least 30 minutes. This goes well with fish and meat dishes.

Root Vegetable Mash
Rotsakspuré

1 Peel the parsnips, carrots and potatoes and chop into cubes roughly ¾ in/2 cm.

2 Bring a saucepan of salted water to a boil and cook the parsnips for about 20 minutes.

3 Add the carrots and potatoes and boil the vegetables for 20 minutes longer.

4 Drain the vegetables and mash them, incorporating some of the cooking water.

5 Enrich the mashed vegetables with the cream and season with salt, pepper, and nutmeg. The mash should not become too fluid. Serve generous quantities of Root Vegetable Mash with all kinds of roast meats.

Serves 4

generous 1 lb/500 g parsnips

2 carrots

4 potatoes

3½ tbsp/50 ml cream

salt

pepper

finely grated nutmeg

*Prep. time: ca. 30 minutes
(plus cooking time)
Per portion ca. 129 kcal/543 kJ
5 g P, 4 g F, 17 g C*

61

Baked White Cabbage
Ugnsbakad vitkål

1 Trim and rinse the cabbage, cut off the stalk, and slice the leaves into thin strips.

2 Bring plenty of salted water to a boil in a large saucepan and cook the cabbage for about 10 minutes.

3 Preheat the oven to 390 °F/200 °C. Dice the bacon and fry in a pan until it is crisp.

4 Remove the cabbage from the saucepan and drain. Combine with the bacon, molasses and Worcestershire sauce. Season with salt, pepper, and caraway.

5 Grease a baking dish and turn the cabbage into it. Pour over the stock. Cover the dish with aluminum foil and bake in the oven for about 50 minutes. Serve with meat and sausage.

Serves 4

½ white cabbage

4 slices bacon

2 tbsp molasses

1 tsp Worcestershire sauce

salt

pepper

1 tsp ground caraway seeds

fat for the mold

1 cup/250 ml vegetable stock

*Prep. time: ca. 30 minutes
(plus baking time)
Per portion ca. 57 kcal/239 kJ
6 g P, 2 g F, 4 g C*

Swedish Pork-filled Potato Dumplings
Kroppkakor

Serves 4

12 medium potatoes

5 oz/130 g fatback

5–6 slices bacon

2 onions

2 eggs

generous ¾ cup/125 g flour

1 tsp salt

3½ tbsp/50 g butter

½ tsp pepper

½ bunch fresh parsley, chopped

*Prep. time: ca. 40 minutes
(plus cooking time)
Per portion ca. 473 kcal/1985 kJ
24 g P, 20 g F, 48 g C*

1 Wash the potatoes and boil them in their skins for about 20 minutes in a little salted water. Drain and allow to cool.

2 Dice the fatback and bacon. Peel and mince the onions.

3 Render the fatback in a pan, then add the onions and bacon and sauté for a few minutes. Season and allow to cool.

4 Peel and mash the cooled potatoes. Add the eggs, flour, and salt to the mashed potatoes and combine into a firm dough.

5 Form the potato mixture into a log and divide into about 12 pieces. Mold each piece into a dumpling around a little of the bacon stuffing.

6 Bring a large pot of salted water to a boil. Put the dumplings in the water. They are cooked when they float to the top, after about 5 minutes. Melt the butter.

7 Serve the dumplings with melted butter and parsley. They go well with fish or meat entrées, or enjoy them as the Swedes do, simply with lingonberry jam.

Stuffed Onions
Fylld lök

1 Peel the onions and cut them in half lengthways. Cook them in a little salted water to al dente (about 8 minutes). Remove from the pot and drain. Reserve the cooking liquid.

2 Rinse the onions in cold water, then carefully separate the large outer layers. Finely chop the inner core. Trim and chop the mushrooms, and mince the sausage.

3 Combine the breadcrumbs, cream, mushrooms, sausage, egg yolk, and chopped onion. Season with salt, pepper, and paprika.

4 Preheat the oven to 430 °F/220 °C. Place a little of the sausage filling on each onion layer and roll up.

5 Generously grease a baking dish with the butter and place the onion rolls in it. Add a little of the onion cooking juices, and bake in the oven for about 30 minutes until the onions are soft inside and crisp outside.

Serves 4

12 large onions

3½ oz/100 g mushrooms

5 oz/130 g sausage meat

2 tbsp breadcrumbs

7 tbsp/100 ml cream

1 egg yolk

salt

pepper

½ tsp sweet paprika

3 tbsp butter

*Prep. time: ca. 40 minutes
(plus cooking and baking time)
Per portion ca. 210 kcal/885 kJ
10 g P, 17 g F, 5 g C*

Potato Salad with Capers
Potatissallad med kapris

1 Wash and cook the potatoes, then peel and dice them.

2 Dice the beets. Add to the potatoes along with the capers.

3 Combine the sour cream with the crème fraîche, mustard, sugar, salt, and pepper and distribute over the salad. Blend well.

4 Finely chop the chives and sprinkle over the salad. Chill well before serving.

Potato Salad with Apples
Potatissallad med äpple

1 Wash and cook the potatoes, then peel and dice them.

2 Trim the leek, remove the dark green parts, and slice the remainder in rings. Heat 1 tbsp of the oil in a pan and sauté the leek for about 5 minutes.

3 Peel, core, and dice the apples. Add the leek and apples to the potatoes.

4 Prepare a salad dressing from the remaining ingredients and toss the potato mixture in it. Chill well before serving.

Potato Salad with Bacon
Potatissallad med rökt bacon

1 Wash and cook the potatoes, then peel and dice them.

2 Dice the bacon. Peel and chop the onion. Render the bacon and then remove from the pan. Sauté the onion in the bacon fat.

3 Make a salad dressing with the vinegar, oil, stock, salt, and pepper and pour it over the potatoes. Combine well, then add the onions and bacon.

4 Sprinkle chopped fresh parsley over the salad. Chill well before serving.

Potato Salad with Chanterelles
Potatissallad med kantareller

1 Wash the potatoes thoroughly and boil in their skins for about 20 minutes. Drain and allow to cool somewhat.

2 Peel the potatoes and slice into rounds. Put them in a bowl. Trim the spring onions and slice into rings. Trim the chanterelles and halve the larger ones.

3 Heat 2 tbsp of the oil in a pan and lightly sauté the spring onions with the chanterelles. Season with salt and pepper.

4 Make a salad dressing out of the remaining oil, the vinegar, stock, sugar, and salt and pepper to taste. Pour over the potatoes.

5 Stir the onions and chanterelles into the potato salad. Finely chop the chives and sprinkle them on top. Chill well before serving. Potato salad traditionally accompanies stuffed eggs and many meat and fish dishes. It also makes a good entrée accompanied by toasted whole-wheat rolls.

Serves 4

1¾ lb/750 g potatoes
1 bunch spring onions
9 oz/250 g chanterelles
5 tbsp oil
salt, pepper
4 tbsp white vinegar
7 tbsp/100 ml vegetable stock
1 pinch sugar
1 bunch chives

Prep. time: ca. 25 minutes (plus cooking and chilling time)
Per portion ca. 191 kcal/802 kJ
5 g P, 6 g F, 29 g C

65

Serves 4

8 medium potatoes

2 tbsp salt

2 tbsp potato starch

freshly ground pepper

2 tbsp chopped chives

3 tbsp butter

2 tbsp oil

*Prep. time: ca. 30 minutes
(plus standing and frying time)
Per portion ca. 212 kcal/891 kJ
4 g P, 7 g F, 32 g C*

Serves 4

8 potatoes of equal size

3½ tbsp/50 g butter

1 tsp salt

2 tbsp breadcrumbs

¼ cup/30 g freshly grated Parmesan

*Prep. time: ca. 20 minutes
(plus baking time)
Per portion ca. 563 kcal/2363 kJ
15 g P, 14 g F, 90 g C*

Potato Pancakes with Chives
Rårakor med gräslök

1   Peel the potatoes and grate them into a bowl. Salt and allow to stand for about 30 minutes.

2   Pour off the liquid from the potatoes. Stir the potato starch into the potatoes. Add some pepper and the chives and mix well.

3   Heat the butter and oil in a pan and make a series of small potato pancakes, frying them until crisp. Serve with a green salad or as the Swedes do, with crème fraîche and caviar.

Hasselback Potatoes
Hasselbackspotatis

1   Preheat the oven to 465 °F/240 °C. Peel and wash the potatoes and cut them in many slices but only partly through. Be sure to keep all the slices connected along the bottom.

2   Melt the butter in a pan and coat the potatoes lightly with it. Reserve some of the butter.

3   Place the potatoes side by side in a baking dish with the cut side upwards. Sprinkle with the salt and bake in the oven for about 30 minutes, occasionally brushing with butter.

4   After 30 minutes, sprinkle the breadcrumbs and remaining butter on the potatoes and bake 10 minutes longer. Then sprinkle with the cheese and bake 5 more minutes until the cheese is melted and nicely brown.

Mushroom & Vegetable Gratin
Svamp-och grönsakgratin

1 Preheat the oven to 340 °F/175 °C.

2 Trim the broccoli and divide into rosettes. Peel the carrots and slice into disks. Cook the vegetables until al dente in a little salted water. Drain.

3 Heat the butter in a pan. Trim and halve the mushrooms and sauté them in the butter.

4 Dust the mushrooms with the flour, then stir in the milk and cream and allow to thicken. Season to taste with the salt and pepper.

5 Place the vegetables in a greased baking dish. Pour the mushroom cream over them and sprinkle with the cheese. Put into the oven and bake for about 8 minutes. This dish goes well with roast meats or fish, or may be served as a meal in itself.

Serves 4

9 oz/250 g broccoli

9 oz/250 g carrots

2 tbsp butter

7 oz/200 g mushrooms

2 tbsp flour

⅔ cup/150 ml milk

⅔ cup/150 ml cream

1 tsp salt

pepper

fat for the baking dish

2 tbsp freshly grated Parmesan

Prep. time: ca. 20 minutes (plus cooking and baking time) Per portion ca. 224 kcal/943 kJ 7 g P, 18 g F, 8 g C

69

Jansson's Temptation
Janssons frestelse

1 Peel the potatoes and cut them into matchsticks. Place in a bowl of cold water to extract the starch.

2 Preheat the oven to 430 °F/220 °C. Peel and roughly chop the onions. Grease a baking dish.

3 Remove the potatoes from the water and pat dry. Remove the anchovy fillets from the tin and drain; reserve the anchovy marinade. Halve the larger anchovies.

4 Place half the potatoes in the baking dish. Cover with the onions, then a layer of anchovy fillets. Cover the anchovy fillets with the rest of the potatoes.

5 Pour the anchovy marinade and half the cream over the mixture. Then sprinkle with the breadcrumbs and dot with butter. Bake for 50–60 minutes in the oven. After 30 minutes, pour in the rest of the cream.

Serves 4

8 medium potatoes

2 onions

fat for the baking dish

10 anchovy fillets with marinade (from a tin)

1 cup/250 ml cream

scant 1 cup/100 g bread-crumbs

2 tbsp butter

Prep. time: ca. 20 minutes (plus baking time) Per portion ca. 428 kcal/1796 kJ 8 g P, 27 g F, 37 g C

Meat & Poultry

This chapter presents a selection of classic and popular meat dishes, from four variations of *Pytt i Panna* — literally "put in the pan" — to the traditional Christmas Ham with its honey crust. Prominent among these are the delightful meatballs known as *Köttbullar*, but the list also includes delicious roasts, steaks and roulades as well as reindeer specialities.

Serves 4

6–8 potatoes boiled
in their skins

1 red pepper

1 green pepper

1 onion

24 small meatballs

oil for frying

*Prep. time: ca. 30 minutes
(plus cooking time)
Per portion ca. 413 kcal/1733 kJ
23 g P, 19 g F, 37 g C*

Meatball Kebabs
Grillspett

1 Slice the potatoes. Trim, halve, and core the peppers,
then cut them into large pieces. Peel and quarter the onion.

2 Alternate the meatballs, potatoes, onions, and peppers
on wood or metal skewers.

3 Coat the completed kebabs with a little oil and grill them
or fry in a pan. Serve with a green salad.

Meatballs
Köttbullar

1 Peel and chop the onion. Melt the butter in a pan
and sauté the onion.

2 Thoroughly combine the meat with the egg and
breadcrumbs, then mix in the onion.

3 Season the meat mixture with salt and pepper and knead
to a smooth mass. Add enough milk to keep it supple.

4 Finely chop the parsley and stir it into the meat mixture.
With damp hands, form small balls from the mass.

5 Heat the butter or lard in a pan and brown the meatballs
on all sides. Serve with rice.

Serves 4

1 onion

1 tbsp butter

generous 1 lb/500 g
mixed ground meat,
such as beef and veal

1 egg

2¼ cups/250 g bread-
crumbs

salt

pepper

1 cup/250 ml milk

½ bunch parsley

2 tbsp/30 g butter or lard

*Prep. time: ca. 20 minutes
(plus browning time)
Per portion ca. 667 kcal/2804 kJ
34 g P, 37 g F, 51 g C*

Reindeer Burgers
Hamburgare på renfärs

1 Combine the meat with the egg, breadcrumbs, salt and pepper, and knead to a firm mass.

2 Form 4 patties, pressing them flat.

3 Heat the butter or lard in a pan and cook the burgers until brown on both sides (about 8 minutes).

4 Halve the hamburger buns and toast them. Then place a lettuce leaf on each of the bottom halves.

5 Remove the burgers from the pan and place one on each of the buns.

6 Slice the tomatoes and cut the pickles into fine strips. Arrange on the burgers, then top with fried onions.

7 Spread mustard on the upper halves of the buns and place on top of the burgers. Tomato salad goes well with these.

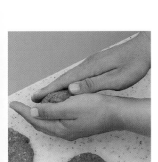

Serves 4

14 oz/400 g
ground reindeer meat

1 egg

7 tbsp/50 g breadcrumbs

salt

pepper

3 tbsp butter or lard

4 hamburger buns

4 lettuce leaves

2 tomatoes

2 pickles

2 tbsp dried fried onions

2 tsp mustard

*Prep. time: ca. 20 minutes
(plus cooking time)
Per portion ca. 353 kcal/1481 kJ
27 g P, 12 g F, 35 g C*

75

Beef Patties
Pannbiff med lök

1 Combine the meats with the salt and breadcrumbs in a bowl to form a smooth mixture.

2 Add the milk and about ¾ cup/200 ml water to the meat mixture, then season to taste with the spices. The mixture should remain firm.

3 Form into patties. Tip the flour into a bowl and coat the patties in it on both sides.

4 Heat the butter in a pan and fry the patties until they are crisp and brown. Remove from the pan and set aside.

5 Peel the onion and slice into rings. Sauté them in the meat fat until transparent. Pour in a little water and reduce to make a sauce. Season with salt and pepper. Hasselback Potatoes go well with these Beef Patties.

Serves 4

9 oz/250 g ground beef

9 oz/250 g sausage meat

1 tsp salt

3 tbsp breadcrumbs

1 cup/250 ml milk

salt, pepper

finely grated nutmeg

1 pinch ginger

⅔ cup/100 g flour

5 tbsp butter

1 onion

*Prep. time: ca. 20 minutes
(plus frying time)
Per portion ca. 708 kcal/2972 kJ
30 g P, 55 g F, 25 g C*

Serves 4

1 white cabbage

¾ cup/150 g
short grain rice

14 oz/400 g ground beef

1 egg

7 tbsp/50 g breadcrumbs

7 tbsp/100 ml cream

4 tbsp each, chopped
fresh parsley, lovage

salt, pepper

2–3 tbsp butter,
plus to grease the dish

2 tbsp corn syrup

1¼ cups/300 ml
vegetable stock

*Prep. time: ca. 30 minutes
(plus cooking and baking time)
Per portion ca. 635 kcal/2667 kJ
25 g P, 40 g F, 44 g C*

Cabbage Roulades
Kåldolmar

1 Remove the outer leaves from the cabbage and cut out the stalk. Separate the remaining cabbage leaves and cook in lightly salted water for about 5 minutes. Remove and rinse in cold water. Reserve the cooking water.

2 Cook the rice in water until just done (about 15 minutes). Drain and allow to cool.

3 Combine the meat with the egg, breadcrumbs, cream, herbs, salt, and pepper. Add the rice and knead briefly to form a paste.

4 Fill each cabbage leaf with some of the meat mixture and roll into a bundle. Preheat the oven to 440 °F/225 °C.

5 Heat the butter in a frying pan, add the corn syrup, and cook the cabbage roulades with the seam side down until that side is brown. Then place the cabbage roulades seam-side down in a buttered roasting pan.

6 Pour a little of the reserved cabbage water into the frying pan and scrape up any browned bits, then pour over the cabbage roulades. Bake for about 45 minutes in the oven. Pour on more of the cabbage water from time to time, as needed.

7 Remove the cabbage roulades. Pour the vegetable stock in the roasting pan, scrape up the drippings and season this sauce with salt and pepper. Serve the Cabbage Roulades and sauce with rice or mashed potatoes.

Meatloaf in Pastry
Inbakad köttfärslimpa

1 Make the pastry out of the flour, butter and 3 tbsp cold water and chill in the refrigerator for 1 hour.

2 Meanwhile, combine the ground beef and sausage with the breadcrumbs, egg, cream, and water. Peel the onion, then chop it finely and add to the meat paste. Season with salt and pepper.

3 Heat 1 tbsp of the butter or lard. Slice the chicken livers and sear for about 3 minutes in the hot fat. Remove from the pan.

4 Preheat the oven to 430 °F/220 °C. Roll out the pastry between two pieces of plastic wrap.

5 Form a loaf from the meat paste; put the chicken livers along the center. Place the meat loaf on the pastry.

6 With damp hands, fold the pastry over the short ends, then enclose the long sides. Bake on baking paper in the oven for about 35 minutes. Served with a tossed salad.

Serves 4

generous 2 cups/300 g flour

1 cup/225 g butter

3½ oz/100 g chicken livers

14 oz/400 g mixed ground beef and sausage

7 tbsp/50 g breadcrumbs

1 egg

7 tbsp/100 ml cream

1 onion

salt

pepper

3 tbsp butter or lard

*Prep. time: ca. 30 minutes (plus chilling and cooking time)
Per portion ca. 865 kcal/3633 kJ
34 g P, 52 g F, 65 g C*

Pytt i Panna with Sausage
Pytt i panna på köttkorv

Serves 4

1¼ lb/600 g potatoes

2 tbsp/30 g butter

1 onion, chopped

12 oz/350 g
smoked sausage

⅔ cup/100 g
diced pickled beets

10 tbsp/150 g
crème fraîche

salt, pepper

1 tsp freshly grated
horseradish

*Prep. time: ca. 20 minutes
(plus frying time)
Per portion ca. 468 kcal/1963 kJ
18 g P, 32 g F, 26 g C*

1   Prepare the potatoes as described in step 1, opposite. Heat the butter in a pan and fry the potatoes and onion until crisp.

2   Chop the sausage into bite-sized chunks and combine with the potatoes in the pan. Cook together for a few minutes.

3   Drain the beets and stir into the crème fraîche.

4   Add the crème fraîche to the pan, heat through briefly, and season with salt and pepper. Serve the hash sprinkled with the grated horseradish.

Pytt i Panna with Roast Meat
Pytt i panna på stekrester

Serves 4

1¼ lb/600 g potatoes

2 tbsp/30 g butter

1 onion, chopped

12 oz/350 g
any roast meat

⅔ cup/100 g
diced pickled beets

10 tbsp/150 g
crème fraîche

salt, pepper

*Prep. time: ca. 20 minutes
(plus frying time)
Per portion ca. 320 kcal/1344 kJ
21 g P, 14 g F, 26 g C*

1   Prepare the potatoes as described in step 1, opposite. Heat the butter in a pan and fry the potatoes and onion until crisp.

2   Dice the meat and add it to the pan with the potatoes. Cook together for a few minutes.

3   Drain the beets and stir them into the crème fraîche. Add the crème fraîche to the pan, heat through briefly, and season with salt and pepper before serving.

Pytt i Panna with Anchovies
Pytt i panna med ansjovis

Serves 4

1¼ lb/600 g potatoes

2 tbsp/30 g butter

1 onion, chopped

12 oz/350 g ground beef

salt, pepper

4 anchovy fillets

⅔ cup/100 g
diced pickled beets

10 tbsp/150 g
crème fraîche

*Prep. time: ca. 20 minutes
(plus browning time)
Per portion ca. 375 kcal/1575 kJ
26 g P, 19 g F, 24 g C*

1   Prepare the potatoes as described in step 1, opposite. Heat the butter in a pan and fry the potatoes and chopped onion until they are crisp.

2   Brown the ground beef in a second pan for about 7 minutes, then season. Chop the anchovies finely and stir them in.

3   Stir the beets into the crème fraîche and season with salt and pepper. Top the potatoes with the crème fraîche sauce and ground beef mixture.

Pytt i Panna with Boiled Ham
Pytt i panna på kokt skinka

1 Wash the potatoes and boil them in their skins for about 20–25 minutes. Drain them, peel while still warm, and allow to cool. Then slice the potatoes.

2 Peel and dice the onions. Chop the pickles and ham into small cubes as well.

3 Heat the butter in a pan and fry the potato slices with the onions and ham until crisp.

4 Stir the diced beets and pickles into the potatoes.

5 Add the crème fraîche and heat through briefly, then season the dish with salt and pepper to taste. Serve topped with fresh parsley, with tomato salad as a side.

Serves 4

1¾ lb/800 g potatoes

2 onions

3 pickles

11 oz/300 g boiled ham

2 tbsp/30 g butter

⅔ cup/100 g
diced pickled beets

1 cup/250 g crème fraîche

salt, pepper

2 tbsp chopped parsley

*Prep. time: ca. 20 minutes
(plus cooking time)
Per portion ca. 495 kcal/2079 kJ
22 g P, 29 g F, 36 g C*

79

Serves 4

1¾ lb/800 g
pickled pork neck

2 onions

2 bay leaves

6 peppercorns

4 cloves

1 clove garlic

4 allspice berries

*Prep. time: ca. 10 minutes
(plus cooking time)
Per portion ca. 360 kcal/1512 kJ
40 g P, 22 g F, 2 g C*

Boiled Pork Neck
Kokt rimmad fläskkarré

1 Trim the pork neck, rinse briefly, and pat dry. Heat a large pot of water and put the neck in it. Peel the onions and add to the pot with the bay leaves, peppercorns, and cloves.

2 Peel and crush the garlic. Crush the allspice berries coarsely and add them to the pot along with the garlic.

3 Bring the water to a boil and simmer the pork neck for about 1 hour 30 minutes over low heat. Carve the meat into slices and serve with cabbage or sauerkraut and parsley potatoes.

Boiled Pork Knuckle
Kokt fläsklägg

1 Place the pork knuckle in a large pot, cover it with water, and add salt. Bring to a boil, then skim off the foam. Trim and finely chop the soup vegetables. Add to the pot with the peppercorns and bay leaf. Salt again, and simmer for about 1 hour.

2 Meanwhile, peel the carrots and potatoes and chop them. After the pork has cooked for an hour, add these to the pot and continue to cook for 20 minutes further.

3 Remove the shoulder from the pot and keep warm. Strain the cooking water. Put the vegetables in a bowl and mash them, adding enough of the cooking water to give them the desired consistency. Carve the meat from the bone and serve with the mashed vegetables, mustard, and mashed potatoes.

Serves 4

1 pork knuckle

salt

1 bunch soup vegetables

10 black peppercorns

1 bay leaf

5 carrots

6 potatoes

mustard

*Prep. time: ca. 20 minutes
(plus cooking time)
Per portion ca. 195 kcal/818 kJ
14 g P, 5 g F, 22 g C*

Pork Roast with Horseradish Sauce
Fylld fläskstek med pepparrotssås

1   Rub the meat with salt and pepper. Peel the apple and the onion. Core the apple and slice into thin rings.

2   Put half the lingonberries on the meat, then distribute the apple and onion on top. Roll the roast together and tie with kitchen string. Preheat the oven to 355 °F/180 °C.

3   Heat the butter or lard and sear the meat on all sides until brown, then roast in the oven for about 1 hour 30 minutes. Baste the meat several times with honey and meat juices while cooking.

4   Combine the sour cream, milk, and horseradish with the lingonberry jelly and heat through in a saucepan. Flavor the sauce with lemon juice to taste.

5   Remove the roast from the roasting pan, carve into slices, and serve with the sauce. Try stuffed dumplings with this.

Serves 4

2¼ lb/1 kg pork roast

salt, pepper

1 apple

1 onion

3 tbsp lingonberries or red currants

4 tbsp butter or lard

2 tbsp honey

1¼ cups/300 g sour cream

generous ¾ cup/200 ml milk

3 tsp grated horseradish

3 tbsp lingonberry or red currant jelly

lemon juice

*Prep. time: ca. 20 minutes
(plus browning and cooking time)
Per portion ca. 528 kcal/2216 kJ
34 g P, 38 g F, 13 g C*

83

Royal Pot Roast
Slottsstek

1   Heat the butter or lard in a pan and brown the meat well on all sides. Season with the salt.

2   Peel and chop the onion. Finely chop the anchovy fillets. Coarsely grind the allspice and peppercorns. Add everything to the meat, along with the bay leaf. Pour the stock over it and braise for about 30 minutes.

3   Remove the meat from the pan and keep warm. Strain the meat juices and measure 1¼ cups/300 ml.

4   Bring this amount of the meat juices to a boil in a saucepan. Blend the flour with the cream and incorporate into the meat juice to thicken it. Add the vinegar and molasses. Season to taste with salt and pepper, then stir in the Cognac.

5   Carve the meat into slices and serve with the sauce. Serve simply with lingonberry or red currant jelly and vegetables.

Serves 4

2 tbsp butter or lard

1¾ lb/800 g beef steak

1 tsp salt

1 onion

3 anchovy fillets

6 allspice berries

6 white peppercorns

1 bay leaf

generous ¾ cup/200 ml beef stock

2 tbsp flour

7 tbsp/100 ml cream

1 tsp vinegar

2 tbsp molasses

salt, pepper

4 tsp/20 ml Cognac

*Prep. time: ca. 20 minutes
(plus braising time)
Per portion ca. 373 kcal/1565 kJ
46 g P, 19 g F, 4 g C*

Serves 4

4 thin beef roulades

salt, pepper

6 anchovy fillets

½ bunch spring onions

2 tbsp butter or lard

1 cup/250 ml beef stock

generous ¾ cup/200 ml
dry white wine

2 tbsp flour

7 tbsp/100 ml cream

*Prep. time: ca. 15 minutes
(plus cooking time)
Per portion ca. 663 kcal/2783 kJ
45 g P, 49 g F, 10 g C*

Beef Roulades with Anchovies
Oxrulader med ansjovis

1 Unroll the roulades on a work surface and season the meat with salt and pepper.

2 Finely chop the anchovies. Trim the spring onions and cut them in rings. Distribute the anchovies and spring onions over the roulades and roll up. Pin together with skewers or toothpicks.

3 Heat the butter or lard in a saucepan and brown the roulades well on all sides. Pour in the stock and wine, cover the pan, and braise the meat for about 45 minutes.

4 Remove the meat from the pan and discard the skewers or toothpicks. Keep the meat warm.

5 Strain the meat juices. Blend the flour with the cream and stir into the meat juices over low heat to thicken. Flavor the sauce with salt and pepper and serve with the roulades. Dumplings make a good complement.

Oscar's Veal Roulades
Oscars kalvrulader

1 Pound the roulades flat and halve them. Clean and mince the mushrooms. Crumble the bread. Combine the mushrooms, breadcrumbs, sausage, cheese, and egg and knead to a smooth paste. Mix in the herbs and season with salt and pepper.

2 Distribute the stuffing over the roulades. Roll them up and tie or secure with skewers or toothpicks.

3 Peel the onion and carrot and slice into rings. Heat the butter in a saucepan and brown the roulades well. Add the onion and carrots to the pan and briefly cook together.

4 Add the wine and tomato purée and bring to a boil briefly. Reduce the heat, cover the pan, and simmer for about 40 minutes, adding water as needed.

5 Remove the roulades from the pan and keep warm. Strain the cooking juices and bind with the cornstarch. Serve the veal roulades with the sauce and a green salad.

Serves 4

4 thin veal roulades

1¾ oz/50 g mushrooms

1 slice white bread

3½ oz/100 g sausage meat

1 tbsp freshly grated cheese

1 egg

1 tbsp chopped fresh parsley

1 tsp sage

salt, pepper

1 large onion, 1 carrot

2 tbsp butter or lard

1¼ cups/300 ml white wine

2 tbsp tomato purée

2 tbsp cornstarch

Prep. time: ca. 25 minutes (plus browning and cooking time)
Per portion ca. 328 kcal/1376 kJ 41 g P, 12 g F, 9 g C

Roast Reindeer with Rosehip Sauce
Renstek med nyponsås

1   Prepare the roast reindeer as described in steps 1 and 2 on the opposite page and roast in the oven, basting with butter.

2   Remove the meat from the roasting pan and keep warm. Pour the stock into the pan, scraping up all the meat scraps, and bring to a boil. Tip the sauce into a saucepan.

3   Blend the cornstarch and cream and add to the sauce. Bring to a boil, stirring constantly until the sauce thickens. Blend in the rosehip purée, vinegar, and apple butter. Salt and pepper to taste.

Roast Reindeer with Rowanberries
Renstek med rönnbärssås

1   Prepare the roast reindeer as described in steps 1 and 2 on the opposite page and roast in the oven, basting with butter.

2   Rinse the rowanberries. In a saucepan combine the berries, red wine, vinegar, and a little water. Bring to a boil and simmer for 2 minutes.

3   Remove the meat from the roasting pan and keep warm. Combine the cornstarch with the cooking juices, pour in the stock, and bring to a boil. Tip the sauce into a saucepan.

4   Stir in the cream and the rowanberry mixture, allowing the sauce to thicken slightly. Season with salt and pepper.

Roast Reindeer with Juniper Sauce
Renstek med enbärssås

1   Prepare the roast reindeer as described in steps 1 and 2 on the opposite page and roast in the oven, basting with butter.

2   Remove the meat from the roasting pan and keep warm. Pour the stock into the pan, scraping up all the meat scraps, and bring to a boil. Tip the sauce into a saucepan.

3   Combine the cornstarch with the cream and add to the sauce. Bring to a boil, stirring constantly until the sauce thickens. Add the juniper berries and gin, and salt and pepper to taste.

Roast Reindeer with Red Onions
Renstek med rödlök och lingon

1 Trim the meat of skin and sinews, and rub it well with salt and pepper. Peel the onions and slice into wedges. Preheat the oven to 320 °F/160 °C. Heat 2 tbsp of the butter in a roasting pan and brown the meat all over. Add half the onions.

2 Roast the meat in the oven for about 20 minutes. Baste with 3 tbsp butter during cooking. For very pink meat, cook to an interior temperature of 140 °F/63 °C; for slightly pink meat, cook to 158 °F/70 °C. Then keep the meat warm.

3 Sear the remaining red onions in an additional 2 tbsp butter. Trim the chili and chop it finely. Combine with the lingonberry or red currant jam, lemon juice, and honey and add this mixture to the onions.

4 Carve the meat in slices. Served with stuffed potato dumplings, the remaining melted butter and the glazed red onions.

Serves 4

1¾ lb/800 g
reindeer loin fillet

salt, pepper

2 red onions

10 tbsp/145 g butter

½ chili pepper

5 tbsp/100 g lingonberry
or red currant jam

1 tbsp lemon juice

2 tbsp liquid honey

*Prep. time: ca. 15 minutes
(plus browning and roasting time)
Per portion ca. 450 kcal/1890 kJ
43 g P, 29 g F, 4 g C*

Serves 6

1 salted ham
(approx. 4½ lb/2 kg)

10 allspice berries

10 peppercorns

8 cloves

1 bay leaf

1 egg

1 tbsp mustard

3 tbsp breadcrumbs

2 tbsp honey

*Prep. time: ca. 15 minutes
(plus cooking and roasting time)
Per portion ca. 500 kcal/2100 kJ
73 g P, 20 g F, 10 g C*

Christmas Ham
Honungsgriljerad julskinka

1 Put the ham in a large pot with the fat side up and add water to cover it. Bring to a boil, skim, and add the spices and bay leaf. Cook the ham over medium heat for about 1 hour 30 minutes. Remove the rind carefully and allow the ham to cool in the cooking liquid.

2 Preheat the oven to 390 °F/200 °C. Combine the egg, mustard, breadcrumbs, and honey, and coat the fat side of the ham with it.

3 Allow the ham to brown in the oven. Carve into slices and serve. Mashed potatoes make a good complement.

Roast Pork
Fläskstek

1 Peel the apple and onions and cut into sticks. Preheat the oven to 390 °F/180 °C.

2 Heat 2 tbsp of the butter or lard in a saucepan. Sear the pork in it, then roast in the oven for about 1 hour 30 minutes. Baste occasionally with the pan juices and a little honey.

3 Melt the remaining butter or lard in a pan and sauté the apples and onions. Add the remaining honey and salt and pepper to taste. Serve with mashed potatoes and salad.

Serves 4

1 apple

2 onions

4 tbsp butter or lard

2¼ lb/1 kg roast pork

4 tbsp honey

salt, pepper

*Prep. time: ca. 30 minutes
(plus searing and roasting time)
Per portion ca. 428 kcal/1796 kJ
53 g P, 19 g F, 10 g C*

Reindeer with Dill Sauce
Kokt renkött med dillsås

1 Place the meat in a large pot and cover with water. Wash and trim the soup vegetables, chop them, and add to the meat with the peppercorns. Bring to a boil.

2 Cook the meat over low heat for about 1 hour 30 minutes. Skim off any foam.

3 Finely chop the dill. Melt the butter in a saucepan, stir in the flour, and brown slightly. Pour in the beef stock and stir constantly until the sauce thickens.

4 Add the cream and dill and flavor with the lemon juice, salt, and pepper.

5 Remove the meat from the cooking juices, allow to drain, and carve it into slices. Serve with the dill sauce. Roast potatoes make a good side dish.

Serves 4

generous 1 lb/500 g reindeer roast

1 bunch soup vegetables

8 peppercorns

1 bunch dill

1 tbsp butter

2 tbsp flour

2 cups/500 ml beef stock

1 cup/250 ml cream

1 tbsp lemon juice

salt

pepper

*Prep. time: ca. 20 minutes
(plus simmering time)
Per portion ca. 398 kcal/1670 kJ
26 g P, 32 g F, 3 g C*

Stuffed Chicken
Fylld kyckling

1 Clean and finely chop the mushrooms. Trim the spring onions and slice them in rings.

2 Heat the butter in a pan and sauté the mushrooms and spring onions for about 5 minutes. Season with salt, pepper, and lovage. Allow to cool in the pan.

3 Finely chop the parsley and combine with the sour cream, eggs, and breadcrumbs. Stir into the mushrooms. Preheat the oven to 355 °F/180 °C.

4 Rinse the chicken inside and out, pat it dry, and rub the outside with salt and pepper. Stuff the chicken with the vegetable and sour cream mixture and close the opening.

5 Put the chicken in a roasting pan, then pour over the wine and lemon juice. Roast in the oven for about 1 hour 20 minutes, basting occasionally with the roasting juices. Serve Stuffed Chicken with a crisp salad and roasted potatoes.

Serves 4

14 oz/400 g mixed forest mushrooms

1 bunch spring onions

3 tbsp butter

salt, pepper

1 tsp dried lovage

1 bunch parsley

generous ¾ cup/200 g sour cream

2 eggs

2 tbsp breadcrumbs

1 roasting chicken, approx. 3¼ lb/1.5 kg

generous ¾ cup/200 ml white wine

2 tbsp lemon juice

*Prep. time: ca. 25 minutes
(plus cooking and roasting time)
Per portion ca. 315 kcal/1323 kJ
16 g P, 24 g F, 5 g C*

Roast Goose
Stekt gås

Serves 4

generous 1⅓ cups/250 g pitted prunes

1 goose with giblets (approx. 8¾ lb/4 kg)

salt

pepper

1¾ lb/750 g apples

1 tsp dried marjoram

Prep. time: ca. 20 minutes (plus soaking and roasting time)
Per portion ca. 768 kcal/3223 kJ
26 g P, 48 g F, 57 g C

1 Soak the prunes in water overnight. Rinse the goose and pat it dry. Rub inside and out with salt and pepper.

2 Finely chop the giblets of your choice (such as liver, stomach, and heart). Preheat the oven to 355 °F/180 °C.

3 Peel and core the apples, and cut into eighths. Chop the prunes and combine with the apples, giblets, salt, pepper, and marjoram to make the stuffing. Stuff the goose and sew closed.

4 Roast the goose for about 3 hours, turning it several times during cooking and skimming off the excess fat. Gradually add 2 cups/500 ml water. After 2 hours 30 minutes, increase the temperature to 440 °F/225 °C. After roasting, allow the goose to rest in the oven with the door open for about 15 minutes.

5 Serve the goose with red cabbage and dumplings. Skim the fat from the pan juices and use the juices as a simple sauce.

Duck Breast with Honey-mustard Crust
Knaperstekt ankbröst

1 Remove any skin and sinews from the duck breasts. Rinse them briefly and then pat dry. Score the fat layer several times crosswise.

2 Blend the mustard with 2 tbsp of the honey and a little salt and pepper.

3 Heat the oil in a frying pan and sear the duck breasts on the fat side for several minutes. Remove the meat from the pan and set it aside.

4 Coat the duck breasts with the honey-mustard mixture. Place them under the grill at full heat and broil for about 10 minutes.

5 Bring the remaining honey, the maple syrup, orange juice, and chicken stock to a boil. Mix the cornstarch with a little water and use this to thicken the sauce.

6 Peel and fillet the orange. Serve the duck breasts with the honey sauce, garnished with segments of orange.

Serves 4

2 duck breasts with fat (11 oz/300 g each)

3 tbsp mustard

5 tbsp honey

salt

pepper

1 tbsp oil

3 tbsp maple syrup

3 tbsp orange juice

1 cup/250 ml chicken stock

1 tbsp cornstarch

1 orange

Prep. time: ca. 25 minutes (plus cooking time)
Per portion ca. 405 kcal/1701 kJ
28 g P, 29 g F, 42 g C

Game

A wealth of big game is encountered in the vast stretches of Swedish forest. In addition to reindeer, which is presented in the preceding chapter, Swedish cuisine includes moose and wild boar specialties, and especially small game such as hare and wild rabbit. The many delicious recipes for game birds are also worth discovering.

Serves 4

8 elk medallions

2 tbsp butter or lard

salt, pepper

1 onion

fresh marjoram, thyme

6 tbsp sharp mustard

2 egg yolks

7 tbsp/100 ml
dry white wine

1 cup/250 ml beef stock

7 tbsp/100 ml cream

2 tbsp aquavit

Prep. time: ca. 20 minutes
(plus grilling time)
Per portion ca. 378 kcal/1588 kJ
31 g P, 26 g F, 3 g C

Elk Medallions
Älgmedaljonger

1 Rinse the elk medallions. Heat the butter in a pan and cook the medallions on both sides until medium rare. Remove them from the pan, season with salt and pepper, and set aside.

2 Peel the onion and chop finely. Mince the herbs. Combine the onion, herbs, mustard, and egg yolks, then coat the medallions with it. Put under a hot grill until the top is crisp (about 2 minutes).

3 Combine the meat juices with the wine and stock and allow to thicken. Enrich with the cream and aquavit, and season with salt and pepper. Serve the medallions with the sauce, parsley potatoes, and a full-bodied red wine.

Serves 4

2¼ lb/1 kg boneless
elk meat

½ bunch thyme,
chopped finely

1 tbsp chopped rosemary

2 onions

2 tbsp butter or lard

1 tbsp tomato purée

3½ tbsp/50 ml aquavit

1⅔ cups/400 ml beef stock

1 cup/250 ml
dry red wine

salt, pepper

3½ oz/100 g
sweet chestnuts, chopped

7 tbsp/100 ml cream

2 tbsp cornstarch

Prep. time: ca. 20 minutes
(plus braising time)
Per portion ca. 585 kcal/2457 kJ
52 g P, 35 g F, 15 g C

Elk Goulash
with Chestnuts
Älggulasch med kastanjer

1 Cut the meat into bite-sized pieces and rub with the thyme and rosemary. Peel and chop the onions. Preheat the oven to 390 °F/200 °C.

2 Heat the butter in a roasting pan and sear the meat over high heat. Add the tomato purée and onions, and brown together. Pour in the aquavit, stock, and wine. Season with salt and pepper. Cover the roasting pan and braise the goulash in the oven for about 1 hour 30 minutes.

3 Stir the chestnuts into the goulash. Blend the cream and cornstarch and thicken the goulash with it. Serve with boiled potatoes.

Roast Elk with Apples & Chanterelles
Älgstek med svamp och äpplen

1   Preheat the oven to 345 °F/175 °C. Rub the meat with the juniper berries, salt, and pepper, then roast in the oven to a core temperature of no more than 140 °F/60 °C.

2   Trim and halve the chanterelles. Peel and finely chop the shallots. Heat 1 tbsp of the butter in a pan and brown the shallots and chanterelles in it.

3   Sprinkle the flour in the pan and pour in the cream and stock. Bring to a boil and add salt and pepper to taste.

4   Peel, core, and quarter the apples, then brown them in the remaining butter and add the mulberry jelly.

5   Carve the roast elk in generous slices and serve with the chanterelles and apples.

Serves 4

1¼ lb/600 g elk haunch

1 tbsp juniper berries, coarsely ground

1 tsp salt

1 tsp black pepper

generous 1 lb/500 g chanterelles

2 shallots

3 tbsp butter

1 tbsp flour

1¼ cups/300 ml heavy cream

1¼ cups/300 ml veal stock

2 apples

3 tbsp/60 g mulberry jelly

*Prep. time: ca. 30 minutes (plus cooking time)
Per portion ca. 563 kcal/2363 kJ
34 g P, 43 g F, 12 g C*

Venison Veal with Berries
Hjortkalvstek med bär

1   Bring the red wine, vinegar, lingonberries, juniper berries, thyme, and generous ¾ cup/200 ml water to a boil, then cool. Remove any skin and sinews from the meat. Pour the sauce over the meat and marinate in the refrigerator for 48 hours.

2   Peel and dice the onions, carrots, and celeriac. Remove the meat from the marinade and pat dry. Strain the marinade and reserve both the liquid and the berries.

3   Preheat the oven to 320 °F/160 °C. Rub the meat with salt and pepper and brown all over in the hot butter or lard. Cook the bones along with the meat.

4   Add the vegetables and tomato purée to the meat and heat together briefly. Pour in half of the marinade. Roast the haunch in the oven for about 1 hour 30 minutes, basting from time to time with the pan juices and the remaining marinade.

5   Remove the meat from the roasting pan and keep it warm. Remove the bones from the pan juices. Purée the juices, strain, and blend in the crème fraîche and reserved lingonberries. Simmer for 10 minutes. Serve the meat with sauce, accompanied with cooked red cabbage and dumplings.

Serves 4

2 cups/500 ml red wine

4 tbsp red wine vinegar

1 cup/100 g lingonberries or red currants

5 juniper berries

1 tsp thyme

3¼ lb/1.5 kg venison veal haunch off the bone and the coarsely chopped bones

2 onions, 2 carrots

3½ oz/100 g celeriac

salt, pepper

3 tbsp butter or lard

1 tsp tomato purée

6 tbsp/100 g crème fraîche

*Prep. time: ca. 30 minutes (plus marinating and cooking time)
Per portion ca. 358 kcal/1502 kJ
33 g P, 20 g F, 7 g C*

Serves 4

2 day-old dinner rolls

generous ¾ cup/200 ml milk

4 wild boar roulades (7 oz/200 g each), pounded thin

2 tbsp mustard

4 slices bacon

1 onion

1 egg

1 bunch each fresh parsley and chives, chopped

1 tbsp lingonberry or red currant jam

finely grated nutmeg

salt, pepper

1 bunch soup vegetables

2 tbsp butter or lard

1 bay leaf

1 sprig rosemary

1 sprig thyme

1 cup/250 ml red wine

1 cup/250 ml game stock

7 tbsp/100 ml grape juice

3 tbsp cornstarch

Prep. time: ca. 30 minutes (plus cooking time)
Per portion ca. 448 kcal/1880 kJ
51 g P, 16 g F, 24 g C

Wild Boar Roulades
Vildsvinsrulader

1 Soak the rolls in the warmed milk. Coat the roulades with the mustard and place a slice of bacon on each.

2 Peel and chop the onion. Squeeze out the rolls and combine with the onion, egg, and herbs. Stir in the lingonberry jam and add nutmeg, salt, and pepper to taste.

3 Distribute the herb mixture over the roulades. Roll up and secure with toothpicks. Trim and chop the soup vegetables (onion, carrot, celeriac, celery).

4 Heat the butter or lard in a pan and brown the roulades in it. Add the vegetables and simmer together. Then add the bay leaf, sprigs of rosemary and thyme, the wine, and the stock.

5 Cover the pan and simmer the roulades for about 1 hour 20 minutes. Then remove them from the pan and keep warm.

6 Pass the meat juices through a sieve, return to the pan, and reduce slightly. Combine the grape juice and cornstarch and use to bind the sauce.

Stuffed Elk Haunch
Fylld älgstek

1   Prepare the haunch for stuffing. Rub the meat inside and out with salt, pepper, thyme, and marjoram.

2   Combine the ground beef, 3½ tbsp/50 ml of the cream, the egg, and the breadcrumbs. Season with salt, lemon pepper, and nutmeg. Mix in the parsley.

3   Place the stuffing onto the haunch. Roll it up and secure with kitchen string.

4   Heat the butter or lard in a roasting pan and brown the haunch all over. Trim the soup vegetables and chop. Add them to the roasting pan and cook together with the meat.

5   Pour the wine and stock over the meat. Add the bay leaf, peppercorns, and cloves. Cover the pan and cook in the oven for about 1 hour. Then remove the lid and roast for about 20 minutes longer to brown the top.

6   Remove the meat from the roasting pan and keep warm. Pass the juices through a sieve into a saucepan and reduce slightly over medium heat. Blend in the remaining cream and the rosehip jam. Season with vinegar, salt, and pepper. Carve the elk haunch into slices to serve.

Serves 4

1 elk haunch, off the bone

salt, pepper

1 tsp each dried thyme, marjoram

7 oz/200 g ground beef

generous ¾ cup/200 ml cream, 1 egg

scant 1 cup/100 g bread-crumbs

¼ tsp lemon pepper

1 pinch grated nutmeg

4 tbsp chopped fresh parsley

3 tbsp butter or lard

1 bunch soup vegetables

2 cups/500 ml red wine

1 cup/250 ml veal stock

1 bay leaf, 5 peppercorns, 2 cloves

4 tbsp rosehip jam

3 tbsp red wine vinegar

*Prep. time: ca. 40 minutes
(plus browning and cooking time)
Per portion ca. 678 kcal/2846 kJ
60 g P, 36 g F, 26 g C*

Serves 4

1 tsp juniper berries

4 hare saddle fillets

pepper, salt

3 tbsp butter or lard

1 onion

½ cup/125 ml beef stock

½ cup/125 ml red wine

1 sprig of thyme

2 tbsp orange marmalade

*Prep. time: ca. 15 minutes
(plus cooking time)
Per portion ca. 233 kcal/981 kJ
33 g P, 7 g F, 5 g C*

Serves 4

1 tsp juniper berries

4 hare saddle fillets

pepper, salt

3 tbsp butter or lard

1 onion

5 oz/150 g plums

7 tbsp/100 ml red wine

1½ cups/350 ml game stock

3½ tbsp/50 ml cream

1 tbsp honey

2 tbsp apple vinegar

1 pinch ground cinnamon

*Prep. time: ca. 20 minutes
(plus cooking time)
Per portion ca. 263 kcal/1103 kJ
34 g P, 8 g F, 8 g C*

Serves 4

1 tsp juniper berries

4 hare saddle fillets

pepper, salt

3 tbsp butter or lard

5 oz/150 g hard cheese
(e.g. Greve)

*Prep. time: ca. 10 minutes
(plus cooking time)
Per portion ca. 242 kcal/1019 kJ
42 g P, 8 g F, 1 g C*

Hare Saddle with Orange Sauce
Harsadel med apelsinsås

1   Prepare the hare fillets as described in steps 1 and 2, opposite. Remove from the pan and keep warm.

2   Peel and chop the onion. Sauté in the same pan in the remaining fat and meat juices until transparent.

3   Pour in the stock and wine. Add the thyme, then bring to a boil.

4   Stir in the marmalade and reduce the sauce slightly. Season with salt and pepper. Remove the thyme before serving.

Hare Saddle with Plum Sauce
Harsadel med plommonsås

1   Prepare the hare fillets as described in steps 1 and 2, opposite. Remove from the pan and keep warm.

2   Peel and chop the onion and sauté in the same pan until transparent. Stone the plums, chop them, and add to the onion.

3   Pour in the wine and stock, and simmer until the sauce is reduced by about a third.

4   Add the remaining ingredients and adjust the seasoning of the sauce before serving.

Hare Saddle au Gratin
Ostgratinerad harsadel

1   Prepare the hare fillets as described in steps 1 and 2 on the facing page.

2   Grate the cheese. Place the fillets in a baking dish and cover with the cheese.

3   Set under a hot grill until the cheese has melted.

Hare Saddle with Chanterelle Sauce
Harsadel med kantarellsås

1 Crush the juniper berries in a mortar. Rub the fillets with the juniper berries and ground pepper.

2 Heat the butter or lard in a pan and sear the fillets on both sides for 2–3 minutes. Salt, remove from the pan, and keep warm.

3 Dice the bacon and sweat it in a pan. Peel and chop the onion. Clean and thinly slice the chanterelles.

4 Add the onions and chanterelles to the bacon and sauté together for 2 minutes. Pour in the wine and game stock and bring to a boil. Reduce the sauce by about a third.

5 Stir in the cream, crème fraîche, and sherry. Cover the hare with the sauce and serve with potatoes.

Serves 4

1 tsp juniper berries
4 hare saddle fillets
3 tbsp butter or lard
4 slices smoked bacon
1 onion
11 oz/300 g chanterelles
7 tbsp/100 ml red wine
1 cup/250 ml game stock
7 tbsp/100 ml each cream, crème fraîche
sherry to taste

Prep. time: ca. 20 minutes (plus cooking time)
Per portion ca. 380 kcal/1596 kJ
41 g P, 22 g F, 3 g C

Pheasant with Cabbage
Fasan med stekt kål

Serves 4

4 pheasant breasts

4 pheasant drumsticks

salt, pepper

5 each juniper berries, allspice berries

4 tbsp oil

3½ oz/100 g slab bacon

1 onion

generous 1 lb/500 g white cabbage

1 pinch each sugar, caraway

generous ¾ cup/200 ml vegetable stock

Prep. time: ca. 30 minutes (plus marinating and cooking time)
Per portion ca. 285 kcal/1197 kJ
39 g P, 11 g F, 7 g C

1   Salt and pepper the pheasant meat. Combine the spices with the oil. Rub this into the pheasant pieces and marinate in the refrigerator overnight. Then brown well on all sides in a hot pan. Remove from the pan and keep warm.

2   Render the bacon in a roasting pan. Peel and chop the onion. Fry them in the bacon fat. Cut the hard stalk from the cabbage. Slice the cabbage leaves thinly and add to the onion.

3   Add the sugar and caraway. Pour on the stock and cook the cabbage for about 20 minutes. Serve the pheasant breasts and drumsticks with the cooked cabbage, and potatoes au gratin if desired.

Game Stew
Viltgryta

Serves 4

1¾ lb/800 g any combination of hare, wild boar, elk and venison

3 onions

7 oz/100 g each carrots, parsnips, chanterelles

2 tbsp butter or lard

salt, pepper

1 cup/250 ml game stock

generous ¾ cup/200 ml dry red wine

1 tsp ground juniper berries

2 tbsp flour

7 tbsp/100 ml cream

2 tbsp elderberry jelly

Prep. time: ca. 30 minutes (plus cooking time)
Per portion ca. 340 kcal/1428 kJ
47 g P, 14 g F, 6 g C

1   Cut the meat into bite-sized pieces. Peel, trim, and chop the vegetables; halve the chanterelles. Heat the butter in a roasting pan and sear the meat in it. Season with salt and pepper. Add the onions and braise them together.

2   Add the game stock, wine, carrots, parsnips, and juniper berries to the pan. Simmer the stew for about 20 minutes. Stir in the chanterelles and cook 10 minutes longer.

3   Combine the flour with the cream and use to thicken the stew. Season with salt and pepper, stir in the elderberry jelly, and serve with noodles.

Fish & Seafood

Sweden, a land of extensive rivers, lakes, and territorial waters, is home to many varieties of domestic fish, including herring, salmon, pike, char, and cod. Its culinary tradition is equally rich: fish can be baked, smoked, pickled, marinated, and poached. The variety is endless—and delicious.

Flounder with Mushrooms
Flundra med svamp

1 Rub the fish fillets with salt and sprinkle with lemon juice.

2 Thoroughly clean and then slice the mushrooms. Preheat the oven to 390 °F/200 °C.

3 Grease a baking dish and place the fillets in it. Top with the mushroom slices. Pour the cream over the mushrooms and cover with the cheese.

4 Bake the fish in the oven for about 20 minutes until the cheese has melted and browned nicely. Serve with rice.

Boiled Cod
Kokt torsk

1 Wash, trim, and finely chop the spring onions. In a deep saucepan, combine the spring onions, white wine, 1¼ cups/300 ml water, peppercorns, and salt. Bring to a boil and simmer for about 10 minutes. Then pour through a sieve, reserving the liquid.

2 Place the fish fillets in a large pot and pour on the onion-wine sauce. Simmer over low heat for about 8 minutes.

3 Peel and finely chop the hard-boiled eggs.

4 Garnish the fish fillets with the parsley, eggs, and horseradish and serve with boiled potatoes.

Matjes Salad
Matjessallad

1 Rinse the matjes herring fillets well, and soak them in the milk for about 2 hours.

2 Trim the beans and cook to al dente in a little salted water. Drain and rinse in cold water. Remove the stem base from the tomato. Blanch the tomato in hot water, then peel and dice it.

3 Peel and chop the potato. Peel, core, and finely dice the apples, then sprinkle them with the lemon juice. Peel the onions and slice into rings.

4 Combine the sour cream with the mustard, salt, pepper, and sugar. Stir in the vinegar and parsley.

5 Remove the matjes herrings from the milk. Drain and slice into wedges about 1¼ in/3 cm wide. Combine with the beans, potatoes, and apples.

6 Add the dressing and toss everything well. Garnish the salad with sprigs of fresh parsley and the diced tomato.

Serves 4

8 fresh matjes herring fillets

1 cup/250 ml milk

3½ oz/100 g green beans

1 tomato

1 boiled potato

2 apples

2 tbsp lemon juice

2 onions

1 cup/250 g sour cream

1 tsp mustard

1 pinch each salt, pepper, sugar

3 tbsp vinegar

3 tbsp chopped fresh parsley

*Prep. time: ca. 30 minutes (plus soaking time)
Per portion ca. 398 kcal/1670 kJ
20 g P, 25 g F, 23 g C*

111

Scallop Salad
Kammusselsallad

1 Remove the scallops from their shells and separate the coral from the flesh. Finely chop the scallop flesh and coral. Season with salt and pepper and sprinkle with lemon juice.

2 Bring the fish stock to a boil in a deep pot, add the scallops and coral, and allow to draw briefly. Remove and cool.

3 Clean and mince the porcini. Trim the spring onions and slice into rings. Heat the butter in a pan and sauté the mushrooms and onions briefly. Season with salt and pepper and stir in the dill.

4 For the salad dressing, season the vinegar with salt and pepper, and slowly beat in the oil a little at a time.

5 Remove some of the lettuce leaves and arrange them on a serving dish. Tear the remaining lettuce into bite-sized pieces.

6 Add alternate layers of the scallops, coral, shredded lettuce, and onion-mushroom mixture. Top with the salad dressing and garnish with the chopped chives. Serve with flatbread (see page 136 for recipe).

Serves 4

14 oz/400 g scallops, with coral if desired

salt, pepper

lemon juice

1 cup/250 ml fish stock

14 oz/400 g porcini mushrooms

½ bunch spring onions

3 tbsp butter

1 tbsp chopped fresh dill

1 tbsp white vinegar

3 tbsp sunflower oil

1 small head iceberg lettuce

1 tbsp chives, chopped

*Prep. time: ca. 30 minutes (plus cooking time)
Per portion ca. 209 kcal/878 kJ
13 g P, 14 g F, 9 g C*

Baked Fish
Fiskgryta

Serves 4

14 oz/400 g potatoes

4 carrots

1 leek

4 pike fillets, salt

2 tbsp oil

7 tbsp/100 ml white wine

1 bunch dill

pepper

generous ¾ cup/200 g
sour cream

1 tbsp tomato purée

*Prep. time: ca. 30 minutes
(plus baking time)
Per portion ca. 308 kcal/1291 kJ
33 g P, 9 g F, 20 g C*

1 Peel and slice the potatoes and the carrots. Trim the leek and cut into thin slices.

2 Preheat the oven to 345 °F/175 °C. Rub the fish fillets with salt and cut into generous chunks.

3 Grease a baking dish and add the fish, potatoes, carrots, and leeks in alternating layers. Sprinkle the oil over everything and pour in the wine.

4 Chop the dill. Top the mixture with the dill, salt, and pepper, and bake in the oven for about 35 minutes.

5 Combine the sour cream with the tomato purée to make a sauce to serve with the Baked Fish.

112

Seafood Gratin
Skaldjursgratin

1 Scrub the mussels thoroughly and remove any bits of seaweed. Discard any that are open. Soak the mussels in water for about 30 minutes.

2 Heat the vegetable stock in a large soup pot and boil the mussels in it for about 6–8 minutes. Then remove them and discard any that are still closed.

3 Remove the mussel flesh from the shells. Trim the spring onions and slice into rings.

4 Melt the butter in a pan. Stir in the flour, then add the fish stock and cream, stirring constantly while it becomes thicker and creamy. Season the sauce with the Worcestershire sauce, salt, and pepper. Fold in the shrimp, parsley, and breadcrumbs.

5 Lightly grease a baking dish. Put the mussels in it and cover with the shrimp cream sauce. Place under a hot grill for 2–3 minutes until golden brown. Serve with a green salad.

Serves 4

2¼ lb/1 kg mussels

3¼ cups/750 ml vegetable stock

1 bunch spring onions

⅓ cup/80 g butter plus extra for the dish

10 tbsp/90 g flour

1 cup/250 ml fish stock

1 cup/250 ml cream

2 tbsp Worcestershire sauce

salt, pepper

9 oz/250 g cooked shrimp

3 tbsp chopped fresh parsley

1½ cups/150 g bread-crumbs

Prep. time: ca. 30 minutes (plus cooking time)
Per portion ca. 708 kcal/2972 kJ
36 g P, 40 g F, 53 g C

Serves 4

4 salmon fillets,
4½ oz/125 g

salt, pepper, 1 lemon

1 cup/100 g breadcrumbs

½ cup/60 g
ground almonds

8 tbsp/120 g butter

1¼ cups/300 ml fish stock

3½ oz/100 g shrimp

2 tbsp/20 g mustard seed

2 tbsp each cornstarch,
slivered almonds

*Prep. time: ca. 25 minutes
(plus cooking time)
Per portion ca. 523 kcal/2195 kJ
35 g P, 33 g F, 22 g C*

Salmon in Almond Crust
Mandelpanerad lax

1 Rub the fish fillets with salt and pepper. Wash the lemon in hot water and cut into eight wedges.

2 Combine the breadcrumbs with the ground almonds. Pack onto the upper side of each fish fillet.

3 Heat 2 tbsp/30 g of the butter in a pan and cook the salmon pieces as described in step 5, opposite.

4 Prepare the sauce as described in step 3, opposite. Serve the salmon fillets covered with the sauce, garnished with the slivered almonds and lemon wedges.

Serves 4

4 salmon fillets,
4½ oz/125 g

salt, pepper

1 cup/100 g breadcrumbs

2 tbsp sweet paprika

8 tbsp/120 g butter

1¼ cups/300 ml fish stock

3½ oz/100 g shrimp

2 tbsp/20 g mustard seed

2 tbsp cornstarch

*Prep. time: ca. 25 minutes
(plus cooking time)
Per portion ca. 438 kcal/1838 kJ
32 g P, 25 g F, 21 g C*

Salmon in Paprika Crust
Paprikapanerad lax

1 Rub the fish fillets with salt and pepper.

2 Combine the breadcrumbs and paprika. Pack onto the upper side of each fish fillet.

3 Heat 2 tbsp/30 g of the butter in a pan and cook the salmon pieces in it as described in step 5, opposite.

4 Prepare the sauce as described in step 3, opposite. Serve the salmon fillets with rice or potatoes.

Serves 4

⅔ cup/100 g sesame seeds

2 eggs, beaten

salt, pepper

4 salmon fillets,
4½ oz/125 g each

3 tbsp flour

8 tbsp/120 g butter

1¼ cups/300 ml fish stock

3½ oz/100 g shrimp

2 tbsp/20 g mustard seed

2 tbsp cornstarch

*Prep. time: ca. 25 minutes
(plus cooking time)
Per portion ca. 540 kcal/2268 kJ
37 g P, 42 g F, 5 g C*

Salmon in Sesame Crust
Sesampanerad lax

1 Toast the sesame seeds in a dry pan. Whisk the eggs and season with salt and pepper.

2 Dip the salmon fillets first in the flour, then in the eggs. Pack with the sesame seeds.

3 Heat 2 tbsp/30 g of the butter in a pan and cook the salmon pieces as described in step 5, opposite.

4 Prepare the sauce as described in step 3, opposite. Serve the salmon fillets with the sauce and potatoes or rice.

Salmon with Dill & Lemon
Lax med dill och citron

1   Blot the fish fillets and rub with salt and pepper. Finely chop the dill and combine it with the lemon zest and breadcrumbs. Pack this mixture onto the upper side of the fish fillets.

2   Cook the beets in their peel in salted water, then cool. Peel and cook the potatoes.

3   For the sauce, bring the fish stock to a boil. Chop the shrimp and add it to the stock with the mustard seed. Simmer until the mustard seeds are soft. Whisk the cornstarch into the sauce, then add 6 tbsp/90 g of the butter, stirring constantly. Season to taste with salt and pepper.

4   Peel the beets and cut them into small pieces. Heat 2 tbsp/30 g of the butter in a pan and briefly sauté the beets.

5   Heat the remaining 2 tbsp/30 g butter in a second pan and fry the salmon fillets, starting with the coated side upwards. Turn them over and cook the other side.

6   Serve the salmon with the sauce, beets, and potatoes.

Serves 4

4 salmon fillets, 4½ oz/125 g each

salt, pepper

2 bunches dill

zest of 1 untreated lemon

1 cup/100 g breadcrumbs

14 oz/400 g beets

1¾ lb/750 g potatoes

1¼ cups/300 ml fish stock

3½ oz/100 g shrimp

2 tbsp/20 g mustard seed

2 tbsp cornstarch

10 tbsp/150 g butter

Prep. time: ca. 25 minutes (plus cooking time)
Per portion ca. 503 kcal/2110 kJ 34 g P, 24 g F, 37 g C

Fried Herring
Stekt sill

Serves 4

8 young herrings, gutted and cleaned

juice of 1 lemon

8 sprigs of thyme

⅔ cup/100 g flour

salt

pepper

7 tbsp/100 ml oil

Prep. time: ca. 15 minutes (plus frying time)
Per portion ca. 485 kcal/2037 kJ
30 g P, 33 g F, 18 g C

1 Sprinkle the herrings with the lemon juice. Put a sprig of thyme inside each fish.

2 Preheat the oven to a slow setting (285 °F/140 °C).

3 Season the flour with salt and pepper and spread it on a large plate. Coat the herrings in the flour, turning them several times. Shake off the excess flour.

4 Heat the oil in a large pan and brown the herrings one at a time for 3–4 minutes on each side. Remove from the pan and keep warm in the oven while frying the remaining herrings. Serve with potato salad.

Herring in Vinegar
Ättiksströmming

Serves 4

⅓ cup/75 ml white vinegar

3½ tbsp/50 g sugar

4 pink peppercorns

1 bay leaf

10 Baltic herrings

salt, pepper

1 bunch fresh dill, chopped

2 tbsp butter

1 red onion

Prep. time: ca. 20 minutes (plus frying and marinating time)
Per portion ca. 234 kcal/983 kJ
31 g P, 5 g F, 15 g C

1 Bring the vinegar to a boil with 1¼ cups/300 ml water. Add the sugar, peppercorns, and bay leaf.

2 Wash the Baltic herrings, remove the heads, and open the fish flat. Season the inside with salt and pepper, and cover generously with about a third of the fresh dill.

3 Close the fish. Heat the butter in a pan and fry the herrings until golden brown.

4 Peel the onion and slice into rings. In a high-sided dish, place alternate layers of the herrings, onions, and dill, then cover with the vinegar marinade. Chill overnight. Herring in Vinegar is traditionally eaten with roast potatoes or warm potato salad.

Steamed Haddock with Vegetables
Kokt kolja på grönsaksbädd

1 Peel the shallots and potatoes. Trim and peel the carrot, celeriac, and other soup vegetables as needed. Halve the shallots, and slice or dice all the vegetables.

2 Blanch the tomatoes and remove their skins and stem bases. Quarter the tomatoes. Dice the bacon.

3 Heat the butter in a large pan and fry the bacon. Add the vegetables and sauté them at the same time. Season with salt and pepper. Add the bay leaves and pour in the wine and fish stock.

4 Rub the haddock with salt and pepper, and sprinkle with the lemon juice. Add to the pan and cover with the vegetables. Cover the pan and cook for about 35 minutes over low heat. Remove the bay leaves.

5 Chop the dill and sprinkle it over the haddock. Serve Steamed Haddock accompanied with rice.

Serves 4

5 shallots

2 potatoes

vegetables for soup: carrot, celeriac, celery, onion, etc.

4 tomatoes

4 slices smoked bacon

3 tbsp butter

salt

pepper

2 bay leaves

½ cup/125 ml dry white wine

1⅔ cups/400 ml fish stock

1¾ lb/800 g haddock

juice of 1 lemon

½ bunch dill

Prep. time: ca. 30 minutes (plus frying and cooking time) Per portion ca. 293 kcal/1229 kJ 43 g P, 7 g F, 13 g C

119

Baked Pike
Ugnsbakad gädda

1 Cook the rice in lightly salted water for about 15 minutes. Drain and set aside.

2 Peel the cucumber and remove the seeds with a spoon. Dice the flesh. Put the diced cucumber in a dish and salt to draw out water. Discard the liquid afterwards and pat the cucumber dry.

3 Hard boil the eggs, then peel and chop them. Peel and dice the onion. Wash, dry, and chop the chives.

4 Heat a little of the butter in a pan and sauté the cucumbers and onions in it. Then combine them in a bowl with the eggs, rice, parsley, chives, and cream. Season with salt and pepper.

5 Preheat the oven to 355 °F/180 °C. Rub the fish with salt inside and out, and fill with the rice mixture. Seal with toothpicks.

6 Melt the remaining butter in a soup pot and brown the fish well on both sides. Then cover with the breadcrumbs and bake for about 40 minutes in the oven. Serve Baked Pike with potato salad or crisp bread and a side dish of coleslaw.

Serves 4

½ cup/100 g rice

salt

1 cucumber

2 eggs

1 onion

½ bunch chives

⅔ cup/150 g butter

½ bunch parsley

3 tbsp cream

pepper

1 small pike

1 cup/100 g breadcrumbs

Prep. time: ca. 30 minutes (plus cooking and baking time) Per portion ca. 558 kcal/2342 kJ 112 g P, 37 g F, 40 g C

Blackened Herrings
Sotare

Serves 4

2¼ lb/1 kg herrings

salt, oil

2 pickles

1 tsp capers

½ bunch parsley

½ bunch dill

½ bunch chervil

2 sprigs tarragon

6 tbsp/100 g sour cream

3 tbsp/50 g mayonnaise

pepper, sugar

Prep. time: ca. 20 minutes
(plus grilling time)
Per portion ca. 453 kcal/1900 kJ
47 g P, 28 g F, 3 g C

1 Gut and wash the herrings, pat dry, and remove the heads. Rub the fish inside and out with salt and coat generously with oil.

2 Place the fish side by side under the broiler or in the oven, and broil on both sides until the skins become black.

3 Shock the broiled fish in cold salted water, then remove the blackened skins.

4 For the remoulade, dice the pickles. Chop the capers and finely chop the herbs.

5 Blend everything in a bowl with the sour cream and mayonnaise, and season with salt, pepper and sugar to taste.

6 Serve the blackened herrings with the remoulade sauce and a green salad.

Two-fish Terrine
Terrin på två sorters fisk

1 Cut the salmon fillet into very small cubes. Trim the asparagus, peel, and cut into pieces. Cook the asparagus in a little salted water until it is tender but still firm.

2 Put the bass fillet through a blender or food processor, then combine with the egg, cream, salt, and pepper. Fold in the chervil, diced salmon, and asparagus pieces. Preheat the oven to 345 °F/175 °C.

3 Grease a mold and fill with the fish mixture. Smooth the surface with a spatula. Cover with aluminum foil, place in a water bath, and bake in the oven for about 1 hour.

4 Remove the terrine from the oven and cool. Slide the terrine out of its mold and cut into slices.

5 For the sauce, blend the remaining ingredients together. Serve with the mayonnaise sauce and roast potatoes.

Serves 4

1 lb/450 g salmon fillet

9 oz/250 g asparagus

14 oz/400 g
sea bass fillet

1 egg

1¼ cups/300 ml cream

salt, pepper

1 tbsp chopped
fresh chervil

3 tbsp chopped fresh dill

3 tbsp chopped
fresh parsley

generous ¾ cup/200 g
sour cream

6 tbsp/100 g mayonnaise

2 tbsp lemon juice

*Prep. time: ca. 30 minutes
(plus baking and chilling time)
Per portion ca. 733 kcal/3076 kJ
47 g P, 58 g F, 7 g C*

Cod with Parsley Sauce
Torsk med persiljesås

Serves 4

1¼ lb/600 g cod fillets

1½ tbsp butter

2 tbsp flour

1½ cups/350 ml fish stock

2 tbsp chopped fresh parsley

salt, pepper

Prep. time: ca. 20 minutes (plus cooking time)
Per portion ca. 163 kcal/685 kJ
27 g P, 5 g F, 2 g C

1   Prepare the fish fillets with the first four ingredients listed in the recipe opposite as described in steps 1 and 2.

2   Melt the butter in a saucepan, then make a roux by blending in the flour and stirring vigorously.

3   Whisk in the fish stock and simmer the sauce for about 10 minutes until slightly thickened. Finally, stir in the chopped parsley and season with salt and pepper.

4   Top the fish fillets with the parsley sauce and serve.

Cod with Curry Sauce
Torsk med currysås

Serves 4

1¼ lb/600 g cod fillets

1½ tbsp butter

2 tbsp flour

1½ tsp curry powder

2 tbsp/30 ml fish stock

1 egg yolk

⅔ cup/150 ml cream

salt, pepper

dry-roasted slivered almonds for garnish

Prep. time: ca. 20 minutes (plus cooking time)
Per portion ca. 318 kcal/1334 kJ
29 g P, 22 g F, 2 g C

1   Prepare the fish fillets with the first four ingredients listed in the recipe opposite as described in steps 1 and 2.

2   For the sauce, heat the butter in a saucepan, then make a roux by blending in the flour and curry powder. Stir vigorously.

3   Stir in the fish stock and simmer the sauce for 2 minutes. Remove from the heat and add the egg yolk, cream, and salt and pepper to taste.

4   Arrange the fish fillets on plates with rice. Accompany with the sauce and and sprinkle on roasted almonds, if desired.

Cod with Herb-mustard Sauce
Torsk med ört- och senapssås

Serves 4

1¼ lb/600 g cod fillets

1 tbsp sugar

2 tbsp malt vinegar

2 tbsp mild mustard

½ bunch fresh herbs (e.g. dill, chives, chervil, parsley), chopped

7 tbsp sunflower oil

salt, pepper

Prep. time: ca. 20 minutes (plus cooking time)
Per portion ca. 145 kcal/607 kJ
26 g P, 4 g F, 2 g C

1   Prepare the fish fillets with the first four ingredients listed in the recipe opposite as described in steps 1 and 2.

2   Combine the sugar, vinegar, mustard, and chopped herbs in a bowl. Add the oil drop by drop, whisking vigorously. Season to taste with salt and pepper.

3   Serve the fillets with the herb-mustard sauce.

Cod with Horseradish
Kokt torsk med pepparrot

1 Trim and chop the spring onions. Bring the white wine and 1¼ cups/300 ml water to a boil with the spring onions, peppercorns, and salt. Simmer for about 10 minutes.

2 Place the fish fillets in a large soup pot. Pour the wine mixture through a sieve and over the cod. Simmer for about 8 minutes over low heat.

3 Hard boil the eggs (approximately 10 minutes), then plunge them into cold water. When cool, peel and finely dice them. Mince the parsley.

4 Serve the fish fillets with boiled potatoes, and garnish with the parsley, diced eggs, and grated fresh horseradish. Accompany with melted butter.

Serves 4

½ bunch spring onions

generous ¾ cup/200 ml dry white wine

5 white peppercorns

1½ tsp salt

4 cod fillets (approx. 1¼ lb/600 g)

4 eggs

½ bunch parsley

4 tsp grated horseradish

Prep. time: ca. 20 minutes (plus cooking time)
Per portion ca. 240 kcal/1011 kJ
34 g P, 8 g F, 3 g C

123

Serves 4

1 day-old roll

1 generous lb/500 g fish fillet

1 onion

½ bunch parsley

½ bunch dill

2 eggs

salt, pepper

1 tbsp lemon juice

¾ cup/75 g breadcrumbs

butter or oil for frying

1¼ cups/300 ml cream

1½ tsp curry powder

*Prep. time: ca. 25 minutes
(plus frying time)
Per portion ca. 463 kcal/1943 kJ
31 g P, 27 g F, 24 g C*

Serves 4

4 plaice fillets

salt

pepper

1 tbsp lemon juice

4 tbsp flour

1 egg

7 tbsp/100 g butter

14 oz/400 g North Sea shrimp

1 bunch dill

*Prep. time: ca. 20 minutes
(plus frying time)
Per portion ca. 293 kcal/1229 kJ
46 g P, 10 g F, 5 g C*

Fishballs in Sauce
Fiskbullar i sås

1 Soak the roll in warm water. Purée the fish fillet in a food processor. Peel and dice the onion finely. Mince the herbs.

2 Squeeze out the roll thoroughly, and combine in a bowl with the fish purée, onion, herbs, and eggs. Season with salt and pepper.

3 Form about 20 little balls from this mixture and sprinkle them with the lemon juice. Roll the fishballs in the breadcrumbs. Heat the fat in a pan and fry the fishballs for about 4 minutes.

4 Season the cream with the curry powder, salt, and pepper and warm briefly in a pan. Serve the fishballs garnished with the curry sauce and accompanied with rice. These fishballs can also be served with many other kinds of sauces.

Fried Plaice
Stekta spättafiléer

1 Rub the plaice fillets with salt and pepper, and sprinkle with the lemon juice. Dredge them on both sides in the flour. Whisk the egg well and pour into a shallow dish. Coat the floured fish fillets with the beaten egg.

2 Heat half the butter in a pan and fry the fish fillets until golden brown. Remove from the pan and keep warm.

3 Add the shrimp to the pan and heat through in the remaining butter. Chop the dill and stir in.

4 Top the plaice fillets with the shrimp, and serve with the remaining butter (melted). This goes well with boiled potatoes.

Crayfish Ragout with Cucumbers
Kräftragu med gurka

1 Peel and halve the cucumber lengthways. Remove the core. Cut the cucumber into pieces about ⅓ in/1 cm wide. Season with salt and set aside.

2 Drain off the drawn cucumber juices. Pat dry and cook for several minutes in a pan.

3 Peel the spring onions and chop well. Heat the butter in a pan and sauté the spring onions.

4 Dust with the flour, then stir in the wine and crab stock. Bring to a boil and simmer for 5 minutes or until the sauce thickens. Then stir in the crème fraîche gently, and season to taste with salt and pepper.

5 Mince the dill. Add the cucumbers and crayfish to the sauce. Stir in the dill and heat everything through. Season to taste with salt and pepper, and add the aquavit. Accompany with basmati rice.

Serves 4

1¾ lb/750 g cucumbers
salt
½ bunch spring onions
3½ tbsp/50 g butter
3 tbsp flour
1 cup/250 ml white wine
1 cup/250 ml crab stock
6 tbsp/100 g crème fraîche
pepper
1 bunch dill
generous 1 lb/500 g crayfish meat
4 tsp/20 ml aquavit

Prep. time: ca. 30 minutes (plus cooking time)
Per portion ca. 273 kcal/1145 kJ 26 g P, 15 g F, 9 g C

Boiled Crayfish
Kokta flodkräftor

1 Trim and peel the soup vegetables as needed and them all into large pieces. Add the vegetables to a large pot of water, along with the dill and salt.

2 Bring the pot to a boil. Put the crayfish in the water one by one, head first. Return to a boil, then turn off the heat, cover the pot, and leave to draw for about 8 minutes.

3 Remove the crayfish from the pot, drain and allow to cool.

4 Extract the meat by carefully removing the middle part of the tail with the intestine to the rear. Pull off the head and claws with a gentle twist. Turn the crayfish over and break open the tail with the fingers. Remove the stomach, gills and giblets.

5 Spoon out the tail meat. Serve the crayfish meat with remoulade and bread.

Serves 4

vegetables for soup: carrot, celeriac, celery, onion, etc.
1 bunch dill
3 tbsp salt
about 12 live crayfish per person

Prep. time: ca. 30 minutes (plus cooking time)
Per portion ca. 143 kcal/600 kJ 29 g P, 2 g F, 3 g C

Serves 4

2¼ lb/1 kg eel

salt

pepper

1 bunch fresh sage

8 slices carpaccio

2 courgettes

2 carrots

1 small leek

2 tbsp oil

2 sprigs thyme

2 tbsp lemon juice

Prep. time: ca. 30 minutes
(plus cooking and baking time)
Per portion ca. 850 kcal/3570 kJ
52 g P, 70 g F, 5 g C

Eel & Carpaccio Rolls
Ål med skinka

1 Skin the eel and cut into 8 chunks of about 1½ in/4 cm each. Season with salt and pepper. Wrap two sage leaves and a slice of carpaccio around each chunk and seal with a toothpick.

2 Preheat the oven to 355 °F/180 °C. Slice the courgettes thinly, then cut into matchsticks. Peel the carrots and chop into matchsticks. Trim the leek and thinly slice the white part.

3 Heat the oil in a pan and sear the eel for about 3 minutes on each side. Then transfer to a baking dish and bake in the oven for about 5 minutes to finish.

4 Reheat the fat from cooking the eel and sauté the chopped vegetables briefly. Season with salt, pepper, and thyme, and add the lemon juice. Distribute the vegetables on plates with the Eel & Carpaccio Rolls on top. Accompany simply with boiled potatoes.

128

Eel Stew
Kokt ål

1 Gut and skin the eel. Wash thoroughly until the water runs clear. Then cut the eel into small pieces.

2 Put the eel into a large soup pot and add sufficient water to cover it completely.

3 Peel the onion and carrot. Cut the onion into eighths and cut the carrot in thick slices.

4 Add the vegetables, vinegar, bay leaf, salt and pepper to the eel, and marinate the eel for at least 2 hours.

5 Bring the pot to a boil, then remove from the heat. Allow to stand for 20 minutes before serving.

6 Prepare a mustard sauce by whisking together the remaining ingredients, and serve with the eel.

Serves 4

2¼ lb/1 kg eel

1 onion

1 carrot

5 tbsp vinegar

1 bay leaf

salt

pepper

5 tbsp mustard

6 tbsp sunflower oil

1 tsp lemon juice

2 tbsp honey

*Prep. time: ca. 25 minutes
(plus marinating, cooking,
and standing time)
Per portion ca. 730 kcal/3066 kJ
39 g P, 62 g F, 7 g C*

Serves 4

**2 trout, ready to cook
(1¾ lb/800 g each)**

9 oz/250 g boiled ham

1 green pepper

2 onions

1 cup/100 g breadcrumbs

4 tbsp lemon juice

½ bunch dill

**2 tbsp butter
plus extra for the foil**

*Prep. time: ca. 25 minutes
(plus baking time)
Per portion ca. 343 kcal/1438 kJ
42 g P, 9 g F, 22 g C*

Serves 4

**2 trout, ready to cook
(1¾ lb/800 g each)**

5 oz/150 g mushrooms

2 shallots

**5½ tbsp/75 g butter
plus extra for the dish**

2½ oz/75 g shrimp meat

5 oz/150 g crabmeat

*Prep. time: ca. 20 minutes
(plus baking time)
Per portion ca. 338 kcal/1418 kJ
56 g P, 6 g F, 14 g C*

Serves 4

**2 trout, ready to cook
(1¾ lb/800 g each)**

1 onion

**2 tbsp butter
plus extra for the foil**

**1½ tsp each
chopped fresh thyme,
marjoram, dill, parsley**

¾ cup/80 g breadcrumbs

*Prep. time: ca. 25 minutes
(plus baking time)
Per portion ca. 315 kcal/1323 kJ
41 g P, 9 g F, 17 g C*

Trout with Ham Filling
Fjällröding med skinkfyllning

1 Preheat the oven and prepare the trout with salt, pepper, and lemon juice as described in step 1, opposite.

2 Dice the ham. Trim, core, and dice the green pepper. Peel and mince the onions. Combine with the green pepper, breadcrumbs, and lemon juice.

3 Mince the dill and stir it into the filling. Stuff the fish with the mixture and dot with butter.

4 Seal the fish in buttered aluminum foil. Bake in the oven for 30 minutes. Serve with a yoghurt sauce.

Trout with Shrimp Filling
Fjällröding med räkfyllning

1 Preheat the oven and prepare the trout with salt, pepper, and lemon juice as described in step 1, opposite.

2 Trim the mushrooms and finely dice them. Peel and chop the shallots. Heat 2 tbsp of the butter in a pan and sauté the mushrooms and shallots in it.

3 Combine the mushrooms with the shrimp and crabmeat, and season with salt and pepper. Stuff the fish with this mixture and seal with toothpicks.

4 Place the fish in a greased oven dish. Dot with the remaining butter, and bake for about 30 minutes in the oven.

Trout with Herb Filling
Fjällröding med örtfyllning

1 Preheat the oven and prepare the trout with salt, pepper, and lemon juice as described in step 1, opposite.

2 Peel and chop the onion. Heat 1 tbsp of the butter in a pan and sauté the onion until transparent. Add the herbs and breadcrumbs, and cook everything together briefly.

3 Stuff the fish with this mixture, seal with toothpicks, and dot with the remaining butter.

4 Wrap the fish in buttered aluminum foil, and bake for about 30 minutes in the oven.

Trout with Almond & Cheese Filling
Bäckröding fylld med ost och mandel

1 Rub the fish inside and out with salt and pepper, then sprinkle the fish with the lemon juice. Preheat the oven to 355 °F/180 °C.

2 Finely chop the chervil. Grate the cheese. Remove the crusts from the bread slices and dice the bread. Combine some of the chervil (up to 2 tbsp), cheese, diced bread, and almonds in a bowl.

3 Blend the mustard with 3 tbsp of the crème fraîche, then combine with the almond mixture and stuff the fish with it. Seal with toothpicks.

4 Place the fish in a large, greased baking dish. Pour in the wine and dot with the butter. Bake for about 35 minutes.

5 Trim and chop the spring onions. Remove the fish from the baking dish and keep it warm. Transfer the cooking juices to a saucepan, and add water to make 1 cup/250 ml. Blend in the remaining crème fraîche.

6 Simmer gently and allow the sauce to thicken somewhat, stirring occasionally. Season with salt and pepper. Fold in the spring onions and the remaining chervil. Serve half a fish per person, accompanied with tomato salad.

Serves 4

2 trout, ready to cook
(1¾ lb/800 g each)

salt, pepper, juice of
1 lemon

1 bunch chervil

5 oz/150 g mild cheese

2 slices white bread

2 tbsp chopped almonds

2 tsp mustard

generous ¾ cup/200 ml
each crème fraîche,
dry white wine

3 tbsp butter

2 spring onions

*Prep. time: ca. 30 minutes
(plus baking time)
Per portion ca. 530 kcal/2226 kJ
50 g P, 30 g F, 11 g C*

131

Serves 4

12 lettuce leaves,
e.g. romaine, radicchio
or lollo rosso

⅔ cup/150 ml heavy cream

1 tbsp lemon juice

4 tsp horseradish
(from the jar)

12 oz/350 g crabmeat

salt, pepper

8 slices smoked salmon

several sprigs fresh dill

Prep. time: ca. 20 minutes
Per portion ca. 240 kcal/1009 kJ
25 g P, 15 g F, 3 g C

Stuffed Salmon
Rökta laxknyten

1   Wash the lettuce leaves and pat them dry, then arrange on four plates.

2   Beat the cream until it is stiff, flavor with the lemon juice, and gently blend in the horseradish.

3   Stir the crabmeat into the horseradish cream, and season with salt and pepper to taste.

4   Distribute the crab stuffing on the salmon slices. Roll up and seal with toothpicks if needed. Arrange on the lettuce leaves on the plates and garnish with fresh dill.

Shrimp in Dill Cream
Räkor i dillröra

Serves 4

14 oz/400 g peeled,
pre-cooked shrimp

1 bunch dill

1¼ cups/300 ml cream

1 tbsp lemon juice

salt

pepper

2 tbsp sherry

1 lettuce

3½ oz/100 g caviar

Prep. time: ca. 20 minutes
(plus marinating time)
Per portion ca. 398 kcal/1669 kJ
29 g P, 28 g F, 6 g C

1   Wash the shrimp, pat dry, and place in a bowl. Finely chop the dill and add it to the shrimp. Stir in the cream and lemon juice. Let the shrimp marinate for about 3 hours in the refrigerator.

2   Remove the shrimp from the marinade and purée. Return the puréed shrimp to the cream marinade and season with salt, pepper, and the sherry.

3   Arrange lettuce leaves on plates, top with some shrimp cream, and garnish with caviar. Serve with rice.

Breads, Cakes & Co.

Apart from bread specialties such as the well-known crispbread, the Swedish kitchen offers an enticing variety of sweet baked goods. St. Lucia Buns and *Semlor* (Lent buns) are delightful treats, as are an array of other sweet pastries stuffed with cinnamon and nuts, or in savoury variations, with feta cheese or salmon cream.

Makes 10

1 cup/250 ml milk

1 oz/25 g yeast

1 tsp salt

1 tsp ground fennel

½ tsp ground caraway

generous 2 cups/300 g
white flour

2 cups/300 g
whole-grain rye flour

flour for work surface

butter for baking tray

*Prep. time: ca. 20 minutes
(plus rising and baking time)
Per piece ca. 243 kcal/1021 kJ
8 g P, 2 g F, 47 g C*

Mixed Grain Crispbread
Knäckebröd

1   Warm the milk and pour 7 tbsp/100 ml of it into a bowl.
Stir in the yeast and allow to stand for about 10 minutes.

2   Add the remaining milk, salt, fennel, caraway, and both
kinds of flour to the dough and knead well. Roll it into a long strip
on a floured work surface, and divide into 10 equal portions. Form
each into a round bun and allow to rise for 10 minutes. Preheat the
oven to 390 °F/200 °C.

3   Roll out each bun on both sides to form a flat circle
approximately 8 in/20 cm around. Place the bread on a greased
metal baking tray and bake for 10 minutes, until crisp. Crispbreads
are excellent topped with various salads or cheeses.

Swedish Wholegrain Flatbread
Svenska fullkornskakor

Makes 14

2 cups/500 ml milk

3½ tbsp/50 g butter

1 oz/25 g yeast

½ tsp salt

3 tbsp sugar

2 tbsp light molasses

½ tsp baking soda

1 cup/100 g
wholemeal rye flour

3½ cups/500 g flour

*Prep. time: ca. 30 minutes
(plus rising and baking time)
Per piece ca. 171 kcal/719 kJ
5 g P, 5 g F, 27 g C*

1   Warm the milk and melt the butter in it. Pour 7 tbsp/
100 ml of the buttered milk into a bowl and crumble in the yeast.
Stir, add the salt, cover and allow to stand for 10 minutes.

2   Add the remaining milk, the sugar, molasses, baking soda,
rye flour, and ⅔ cup/100 g of the wheat flour to the yeast
mixture. Knead everything thoroughly and let it rise in a warm
place for 30 minutes. Knead in the wheat flour and allow to rest
for another 45 minutes.

3   Divide the dough into 14 pieces and form into little balls. On
a floured work surface, roll the dough balls into flat patties about
5 mm thick. Toss them from one hand to the other to shake off
excess flour. In a medium hot non-stick pan, scorch the flatbreads
one by one, about 3 minutes each side. Cool on a wire rack. Serve
with snacks and hors d'oeuvres, or simply top with butter or cheese.

St. Lucia Buns
Lussekatter

1   Melt the butter in a saucepan. Heat the milk gently in a separate pot.

2   Add the saffron and 1 pinch of the sugar to some of the warmed milk and stir until dissolved.

3   Add the yeast to the remaining milk, stirring until dissolved. Now add the melted butter and the saffron milk, and stir well. Incorporate the remaining sugar and the salt. Sift in the flour. Knead the dough well until bubbles form and the dough comes away from the sides of the bowl. Soak the raisins in hot water for several minutes to plump them.

4   Knead the almonds into the dough and leave to rest in a warm place for about 45 minutes.

5   Preheat the oven to 450 °F/230 °C. Knead the dough again thoroughly. Form it into a long sausage and cut it into 6 in/15 cm lengths. Form each length into an "S" shape. Cross one "S" over another, tuck in the ends, and press together gently.

6   Sprinkle raisins into the gaps and brush the buns with the beaten egg yolk. Place the buns on a greased and floured tray and bake for 7–10 minutes. St. Lucia Buns are traditionally eaten on St. Lucia's Day, December 13th.

Makes 12

⅔ cup/150 g butter

2 cups/500 ml milk

3 pinches saffron

9 tbsp/125 g sugar

1¾ oz/50 g yeast

½ tsp salt

6 cups/850 g flour

¾ cup/100 g raisins

¾ cup/80 g chopped almonds (optional)

1 egg yolk, beaten

*Prep. time: ca. 30 minutes
(plus rising and baking time)
Per piece ca. 394 kcal/1655 kJ
10 g P, 9 g F, 69 g C*

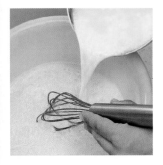

139

Semlor (Lenten Buns)
Semlor med mandelmassa

1   Heat the milk and melt the butter in it. Crumble the yeast into 7 tbsp/100 ml of the milk, stir, and add the salt. Allow the yeast mixture to stand for about 10 minutes.

2   Stir in 1 egg and the sugar. Add the flour and stir gently until the batter becomes elastic (can be pulled into threads). Leave the dough to rest for about 30 minutes.

3   Knead the dough thoroughly once more and form it into 10 round buns. Allow the buns to rest for 30 minutes.

4   Meanwhile, preheat the oven to 375 °F/190 °C. Whisk the second egg. Glaze the buns with the beaten egg and bake for 7–10 minutes.

5   Cool the buns on a wire rack. When cool, slice them in half horizontally and scoop out the centers. Whip the cream. Mix the scooped centers, almond paste, and ⅓ of the whipped cream. Fill both halves of the hollowed buns with the mixture.

6   Sandwich the remaining cream between the bun halves. Dust the *Semlor* with powdered sugar and serve with coffee.

Makes 10

1¼ cups/300 ml milk

3½ tbsp/50 g butter

1¾ oz/50 g yeast

½ tsp salt

2 eggs

7 tbsp/100 g sugar

6½ cups/900 g flour

5 oz/150 g almond paste

1½ cups/350 ml heavy cream

powdered sugar for dusting

*Prep. time: ca. 30 minutes
(plus rising and baking time)
Per piece ca. 610 kcal/2562 kJ
16 g P, 23 g F, 83 g C*

Cream Cake with Berries
Gräddtårta med blandade bär

**Makes 1 cake
(12 slices)**

4 eggs

⅔ cup/150 g sugar

7 tbsp/60 g flour

6 tbsp/60 g potato starch

1 tsp cream of tartar

butter, flour for the pan

1⅔ cups/400 ml
heavy cream

2 tbsp vanilla sugar

generous 1 lb/500 g
mixed berries

*Prep. time: ca. 25 minutes
(plus baking time)
Per piece ca. 250 kcal/1053 kJ
5 g P, 14 g F, 27 g C*

1 Whisk the eggs with the plain sugar in a bowl until frothy.

2 Sieve the flour, potato flour and cream of tartar together and stir into the beaten eggs. Grease a circular springform cake tin and dust with flour.

3 Preheat the oven to 355 °F/180 °C. Pour the batter into the cake tin and bake on the lowest rack of the oven for about 40 minutes. Cool and slice horizontally into three layers.

4 Beat the cream and vanilla sugar together until very stiff. Use half the whipped cream to cover two of the cake layers. Trim, wash and drain the berries, then distribute a third of them over the cream-covered cake layers.

5 Reassemble the cake with the plain third layer on top. Cover completely with the remaining cream. Decorate with berries, a dusting of cocoa powder and chocolate shavings, if desired. Chill the cake before serving it with tea.

Swedish Almond Cake
Mandeltårta

1 Preheat the oven to 390 °F/200 °C. Separate the eggs. Beat 4 egg whites until stiff, gradually incorporating half the ground almonds and ½ cup/110 g of the sugar. Line a springform baking tin with greaseproof paper and pour in the batter. Bake the cake base for about 20 minutes.

2 Make a second cake base from the remaining egg whites, ground almonds and ½ cup/110 g sugar. Allow both cake bases to cool. In a dry pan, toast the slivered almonds until golden.

3 For the butter cream, melt the butter slowly in a saucepan but do not let it overheat. Beat the remaining sugar, the cornflour and the egg yolks with the butter until frothy. Place in a double-boiler and continue to whisk until the cream begins to thicken.

4 Spread butter cream on each cake base and assemble the cake. Cover the sides of the cake with the remaining butter cream and cover with the toasted almonds. Dust with icing sugar. Serve with whipped cream and coffee.

**Makes 1 cake
(12 slices)**

8 eggs

1⅓ cups/200 g
ground almonds

2 cups + 2 tbsp/470 g
sugar

⅔ cup/75 g
slivered almonds

14 tbsp/200 g butter

⅓ cup/40 g cornstarch

powdered sugar for dusting

*Prep. time: ca. 30 minutes
(plus baking time)
Per piece ca. 284 kcal/1193 kJ
8 g P, 27 g F, 4 g C*

Raisin & Nut Pinwheels
Vetebullar med nötfyllning

Makes 15

For the filling:

2 cups/250 g finely ground mixed nuts

6 tbsp/50 g raisins

⅓ cup/75 g sugar

¼ cup/60 ml cream

2 tbsp butter, melted

1 egg yolk

Prep. time: ca. 30 minutes (plus rising and baking time) Per portion ca. 219 kcal/921 kJ 5 g P, 15 g F, 17 g C

1 Prepare the dough with the first six ingredients listed in the recipe opposite as described in steps 1 and 2.

2 For the filling, combine the ground nuts with the raisins, sugar and melted butter. Stir in the cream.

3 Distribute this mixture onto the rolled-out dough and form spiral-shaped buns as described in steps 4–6, opposite. Brush them with egg yolk and bake.

Pinwheels with Salmon Cream
Salta bullar med laxfyllning

Makes 15

⅓ cup/75 g butter

1 cup/250 ml milk

1 oz/25 g yeast

1 tbsp sugar

½ tsp each salt, dried dill

3½ cups/500 g flour

For the filling:

salmon cream (recipe on page 18)

Prep. time: ca. 30 minutes (plus rising and baking time) Per piece ca. 231 kcal/971 kJ 13 g P, 6 g F, 30 g C

1 Prepare the dough as described in steps 1 and 2, opposite, using dill instead of cardamom.

2 Prepare the salmon cream and spread over the rolled-out dough. Then form the spiral-shaped rolls and bake as described in steps 4–6, opposite.

Pinwheels with Cheese
Salta bullar med ostfyllning

Makes 15

⅓ cup/75 g butter

1 cup/250 ml milk

1 oz/25 g yeast

1 tbsp sugar

½ tsp salt

½ tsp ground coriander

3½ cups/500 g flour

For the filling:

7 oz/200 g feta cheese

1 tsp chopped fresh herbs

1 tbsp tomato purée

Prep. time: ca. 30 minutes (plus rising and baking time) Per piece ca. 168 kcal/708 kJ 5 g P, 5 g F, 25 g C

1 Prepare the dough as described in steps 1 and 2, opposite, using cordiander instead of cardamom.

2 For the filling, combine the feta cheese with the herbs and tomato purée.

3 Spread this mixture onto the rolled-out dough. Then form the spiral-shaped rolls and bake as described in steps 4–6, opposite.

Cinnamon Pinwheels
Kanelbullar

1   Melt the butter. Add the milk and warm the mixture gently. Dissolve the yeast in this mixture, then stir in the sugar, salt, cardamom, and almost all of the flour. Knead until the dough is pliable, adding more flour if necessary. Then set the dough aside to rise for 30–40 minutes.

2   Knead the dough thoroughly on a floured work surface and divide into three equal portions.

3   For the filling, melt the butter. Roll out each portion of dough into a thin rectangle and coat with the butter. Combine the cinnamon and sugar and spread it on the dough.

4   Now roll up the dough like a carpet and slice into spirals approximately 1½ in/4 cm thick. Place cut-side down on a metal baking tray. Allow the rolls to rise again.

5   Preheat the oven to 480 °F/250 °C. Brush the pinwheels with the beaten egg and dust with sugar (coarse or granulated).

6   Bake the Cinnamon Pinwheels on the middle rack of the oven for about 5–8 minutes. Remove, cool, and serve with coffee.

Makes 15

⅓ cup/75 g butter

1 cup/250 ml milk

1 oz/25 g yeast

7 tbsp/100 g sugar

½ tsp each salt, cardamom

3½ cups/500 g flour

For the filling:

2½ tbsp/40 g butter

1½ tsp cinnamon

3½ tbsp/50 g sugar

1 egg for glazing

sugar for dusting

*Prep. time: ca. 30 minutes
(plus rising and baking time)
Per piece ca. 224 kcal/940 kJ
7 g P, 8 g F, 31 g C*

Eivor's Orange Cake
Eivors apelsinkaka

**Makes 1 cake
(18 slices)**

⅔ cup/150 g butter

⅔ cup/100 g brown sugar

3 eggs

zest of 2 untreated lemons

5 tbsp/70 ml freshly
squeezed orange juice

scant 1⅓ cups/225 g flour

2 tsp baking powder

butter and flour for the pan

scant 1 cup/100 g pow-
dered sugar

oil, orange food coloring

julienned zest of 1 orange

*Prep. time: ca. 30 minutes
(plus baking time)
Per piece ca. 111 kcal/467 kJ
2 g P, 3 g F, 17 g C*

1   Beat together the butter and sugar in a bowl until fluffy. Add the eggs one at a time and continue beating to a creamy consistency. Preheat the oven to 355 °F/180 °C.

2   Combine the lemon zest, 3½ tbsp/50 ml of the orange juice, the flour and baking powder, and fold into the egg batter. Butter a loaf pan and dust it with flour. Pour the batter into the pan, smooth the top, and bake for about 40 minutes. Remove the cake from the pan and allow to cool.

3   Mix the remaining orange juice and the powdered sugar to make a glaze. Add a few drops of oil and food coloring if desired, and cover the cake with it. Decorate with the julienned orange zest. Serve with coffee or with fruit as a dessert.

Lemon Cake
Jämtländsk citronkaka

**Makes 1 cake
(18 slices)**

3 eggs

3 tbsp sugar

1¾ cups/250 g flour

2 tsp baking powder

zest of 1 untreated lemon

10 tbsp/150 g sour cream

5 oz/150 g cream cheese

butter and flour for the tin

*Prep. time: ca. 20 minutes
(plus baking time)
Per piece ca. 103 kcal/436 kJ
4 g P, 5 g F, 11 g C*

1   Preheat the oven to 355 °F/180 °C. Separate the eggs. Beat the egg yolks with the sugar until foamy. Sift together the flour and baking powder and stir into the egg mixture. Fold in the lemon zest.

2   Blend the sour cream with the cream cheese. Beat the egg whites until stiff and blend them into the cheese mixture. Gently fold into the cake batter (do not stir).

3   Butter a loaf pan and dust with flour. Pour in the batter and bake for about 40 minutes. Do not open the oven door during the first 20 minutes. Serve the Lemon Cake while still warm.

Desserts

Swedish desserts range from *Nyponsoppa*, a delicious Cold Rosehip Soup that is a favorite with children, to Cinnamon Cream, red fruit jellies and rice puddings. Berries (preferably freshly picked) are held in high esteem, and are indispensable for many Swedish desserts. Pancakes are also eaten enthusiastically, and although they are included with desserts here, they are often a meal in themselves in Sweden.

Berry Fruit Salad
Fruktsallad på färska bär

Serves 4

¾ cup/100 g blueberries

¾ cup/100 g strawberries

¾ cup/100 g blackberries

¾ cup/100 g raspberries

1 cup/125 g red currants

2 tbsp black currant jelly

1 tsp Cassis

juice of 1 orange

3 tbsp honey

*Prep. time: ca. 20 minutes
(plus drawing time)
Per portion ca. 97 kcal/405 kJ
3 g P, 2 g F, 15 g C*

1 Hull the berries and strip the red currants. Wash and drain all the berries and place in a bowl.

2 Mix together the black currant jelly, Cassis, and orange juice. Add the honey and beat until creamy.

3 Pour this cream over the berries and fold them in gently. Allow the berry salad to draw in the refrigerator for about 20 minutes. Vanilla ice cream or vanilla pudding and cream goes well with this berry fruit salad.

148

Cold Rosehip Soup
Kall nyponsoppa

Serves 4

9 oz/250 g dried rosehips

4½ tbsp/60 g sugar

1 tbsp cornstarch

1 tbsp honey

juice of ½ lemon

7 tbsp/100 ml
heavy cream

2 butter biscuits
or almond biscotti

*Prep. time: ca. 20 minutes
(plus soaking and cooking time)
Per portion ca. 147 kcal/618 kJ
2 g P, 1 g F, 32 g C*

1 Crush the rosehips in a mortar and soak for 3–4 hours in cold water. Then boil the rosehips gently in the same water for about 30 minutes.

2 Filter the rosehip juices and add enough water to yield 1½ quarts/1.5 liters. Stir in the sugar and return to a boil.

3 Blend the cornstarch in a little water and add to the boiling soup. Stir gently while it thickens, then leave to cool. Season with honey and lemon juice. Garnish the chilled syrup with whipped cream and halved butter biscuits.

Apple Charlotte
Brödpudding med äpple

1 Cut the bread in half diagonally. Combine the milk with the eggs and soak the bread in it.

2 Rinse the raisins in hot water and drain. Preheat the oven to 390 °F/200 °C.

3 Peel, halve, and core the apples, then cut into thin slices. Grease a baking dish.

4 Layer the soaked slices of bread, apple slices, and raisins in the dish. Pour the egg and milk mixture over the top. Sprinkle with the sugar and cinnamon.

5 Dot with the butter, and bake the Apple Charlotte in the oven for about 30 minutes, or until golden brown. Serve while still warm with vanilla sauce or vanilla ice cream.

Serves 4

12 slices white bread

1⅔ cups/400 ml milk

2 eggs

scant 1¼ cups/150 g raisins

3 apples

3 tbsp brown sugar

½ tsp ground cinnamon

2 tbsp/30 g butter plus extra for greasing

Prep. time: ca. 30 minutes (plus soaking and baking time) Per portion ca. 603 kcal/2531 kJ 15 g P, 17 g F, 95 g C

Rhubarb Crumble
Smulpaj med rabarber

1 Combine the flour and half the sugar in a bowl. Grind generous ¾ cup/100 g of the nuts finely, and blend well with the flour and sugar.

2 Slowly rub the butter into the flour and ground nuts until the mixture resembles fine breadcrumbs. Preheat the oven to 390 °F/200 °C.

3 Trim the rhubarb, remove the skin, and chop into small pieces. Combine the rhubarb with the remaining sugar and the cornstarch.

4 Grease a baking dish. Place the rhubarb mixture in it and cover with the crumble topping.

5 Bake the crumble on the middle rack for about 30 minutes, until the topping becomes lightly browned.

6 Chop the remaining nuts and sprinkle over the dessert. Serve Rhubarb Crumble with whipped cream and strawberry sauce, or according to taste.

Serves 4

¾ cup + 2 tbsp/120 g flour

7 tbsp/100 g sugar

1¼ cup/150 g walnuts or hazelnuts

7 tbsp/100 g butter plus extra for the dish

1 lb/450 g rhubarb

1 tbsp cornstarch

Prep. time: ca. 20 minutes (plus baking time) Per portion ca. 400 kcal/1680 kJ 6 g P, 19 g F, 51 g C

Cinnamon Cream with Blueberries
Kanelkräm med blåbär

Serves 4

7 tbsp/100 ml milk

7 tbsp/100 ml cream

1 cinnamon stick

3 egg yolks

2 tsp cornstarch

7 tbsp/100 g sugar

2 cups/300 g blueberries

4 tbsp brown sugar

*Prep. time: ca. 20 minutes
(plus cooking time)
Per portion ca. 270 kcal/1134 kJ
4 g P, 14 g F, 33 g C*

1 Combine the milk and cream in a saucepan, add the cinnamon stick, and bring to a boil. Remove from the heat and set aside to let the cinnamon flavor develop.

2 Combine the egg yolks with the cornstarch and sugar, and stir into the milk mixture. Let the cream simmer, stirring constantly, until it thickens.

3 Hull the blueberries, wash, and drain. Distribute the berries among 4 ovenproof dessert glasses.

4 Remove the cinnamon stick from the cream. Pour the cinnamon cream over the berries and allow to cool. Then top with the brown sugar and caramelize in the oven or under the broiler, or with a blow torch.

Creamed Rice Pudding with Red Berries
Rispudding med kräm på röda bär

1 Cut the vanilla bean open lengthwise and scrape out the mark. Bring the vanilla mark and pod, half of the lemon zest, the salt, and the milk to a boil. Stir in the rice and simmer over low heat, covered, for about 25 minutes, stirring occasionally.

2 Remove the vanilla bean. Soak the gelatine in a little cold water for 10 minutes. Press excess water from the gelatine and stir it into the hot rice with half the sugar. When the gelatine has dissolved, remove the rice from the heat and chill.

3 Beat the cream until stiff. As soon as the rice begins to gel, fold in the cream. Transfer to a large bowl and chill, covered.

4 For the topping, wash the berries and pat dry, halving as desired. Boil together the cherry juice, cinnamon stick, and remaining lemon zest and sugar for 5 minutes. Remove the cinnamon stick. Dissolve the starch in a little water, then stir it in. Remove from the heat, cover, and chill. Garnish the rice pudding with the red fruit topping and a sprig of lemon balm.

Serves 4

1 vanilla bean

grated zest of
1 untreated lemon

1 pinch salt

2½ cups/600 ml milk

6 tbsp/80 g
short grain rice

3 sheets or ¾ envelope
clear gelatine

9 tbsp/120 g sugar

generous ¾ cup/200 ml
heavy cream

1 lb/450 g mixed berries

1 cup/250 ml cherry juice

½ cinnamon stick

2 tbsp cornstarch

lemon balm for garnish

*Prep. time: ca. 45 minutes
(plus cooking time)
Per portion ca. 458 kcal/1922 kJ
8 g P, 21 g F, 57 g C*

Serves 4

2 eggs

1¼ cups/300 ml milk

7 tbsp/100 ml cream

⅔ cup/100 g
whole-wheat flour

1 pinch salt

2 apples

3 tbsp oil

4 tbsp sugar

½ tsp cinnamon

*Prep. time: ca. 20 minutes
(plus resting and cooking time)
Per portion ca. 308 kcal/1291 kJ
10 g P, 17 g F, 29 g C*

Apple Pancakes
Pannkakor med äppelbitar

1   Make the pancake batter as described in step 1, opposite.

2   Peel, quarter, and core the apples. Chop, thinly slice or grate the apples.

3   Stir the apples into the pancake batter and cook the pancakes as described in steps 3 and 4, opposite. Sprinkle the finished pancakes with sugar and cinnamon.

Serves 4

2 eggs

1¼ cups/300 ml milk

7 tbsp/100 ml cream

⅔ cup/100 g
whole-wheat flour

1 pinch salt

12 oz/350 g cherries

3 tbsp oil for the pan

4 tbsp sugar

powdered sugar

*Prep. time: ca. 20 minutes
(plus resting and cooking time)
Per portion ca. 343 kcal/1439 kJ
11 g P, 18 g F, 34 g C*

Cherry Pancakes
Pannkakor med körsbär

1   Make the pancake batter as described in step 1, opposite.

2   Wash and stone the cherries.

3   Cook one side of the pancake, place ¼ of the cherries on it, turn and cook the other side until golden brown.

4   Serve the cherry pancakes sprinkled with sugar and dusted with powdered sugar.

Serves 4

2 eggs

1¼ cups/300 ml milk

7 tbsp/100 ml cream

⅔ cup/100 g
whole-wheat flour

1 pinch salt

4 tbsp sugar

1 tsp ground cinnamon

3 tbsp oil for the pan

powdered sugar

*Prep. time: ca. 20 minutes
(plus resting and cooking time)
Per portion ca. 290 kcal/1218 kJ
10 g P, 17 g F, 25 g C*

Cinnamon Pancakes
Kanelpannkakor

1   Make the pancake batter as described in step 1, opposite. Add in the sugar and cinnamon.

2   Make about 8 pancakes, browning both sides.

3   Dust the pancakes with powdered sugar and serve with fruit compote and whipped cream, or with red fruit jam, as is traditional in Sweden.

Blueberry Pancakes
Pannkakor med blåbär

1 Whisk together the eggs and milk, then stir in the cream. Mix in the flour and salt and stir to produce a creamy batter. Allow the batter to rest for 10–15 minutes.

2 In a cast iron pan, heat 1 tbsp of the oil. Pour in some of the batter and cook for 30 seconds.

3 Cull and rinse the blueberries and drain well or pat dry.

4 Place some of the blueberries on the pancake, allow to settle into the batter, then turn the pancake and cook on the other side until golden brown.

5 Repeat for each blueberry pancake, replenishing the oil in the pan as necessary.

6 Top the pancakes as desired with sugar or powdered sugar, and serve with whipped cream.

Serves 4

2 eggs

1¼ cups/300 ml milk

7 tbsp/100 ml cream

⅔ cup/100 g whole-wheat flour

1 pinch salt

1⅓ cups/200 g blueberries

3 tbsp oil

4 tbsp sugar

Prep. time: ca. 20 minutes (plus resting and cooking time)
Per portion ca. 298 kcal/1250 kJ
10 g P, 17 g F, 26 g C

155

Serves 4

1¼ cups/300 ml
heavy cream

3 eggs

⅔ cup/150 g sugar

3½ oz/100 g cream cheese

mark of ½ vanilla bean

6 butter biscuits
or graham crackers

14 oz/400 g strawberries

Prep. time: ca. 15 minutes
(plus freezing time)
Per portion ca. 735 kcal/3087 kJ
15 g P, 44 g F, 70 g C

Cream Cheese Ice Cream
Glass på färskost

1 Beat the cream until stiff. Separate the eggs and whisk the egg whites until they are stiff.

2 Beat the egg yolks with the sugar and cream cheese until foamy. Blend in the vanilla mark.

3 Carefully combine the whipped cream, egg whites, and the cream cheese mixture.

4 Crush the biscuits with a rolling pin and place the crumbs in one dish or 4 individual bowls. Top with the cream cheese mixture and put in the freezer for 4–5 hours to set.

5 Clean and trim the strawberries and cut into small pieces. Remove the ice cream from the freezer 25 minutes before serving. Accompany with strawberries.

Lingonberry Parfait
Lingonparfait

Serves 4

¾ cup/100 g
fresh lingonberries
(or red currants)

2 egg yolks

3½ tbsp/50 g sugar

1⅓ cups/400 ml cream

sprigs of mint for garnish

Prep. time: ca. 15 minutes
(plus freezing time)
Per portion ca. 330 kcal/1386 kJ
4 g P, 26 g F, 19 g C

1 Cull and wash the lingonberries. Pat them dry, then purée in a blender or food processor. Whisk the egg yolks and sugar until foamy. Combine with the puréed berries.

2 Bring 1¼ cups/300 ml of the cream to a boil. Whisk in the berry mixture, beating vigorously. Allow to cool.

3 Fill 4 dessert cups with the mixture and freeze overnight. Beat the remaining cream until stiff. Garnish with mint and the whipped cream.

Red Currant Compote with Cream
Röd vinbärskompott med grädde

1 Cull and wash the red currants. Drain in a colander. Reserve a few whole red currants for garnish and simmer the rest gently in ¾ cup/200 ml water.

2 After about 10 minutes, stir the cornstarch into a little of the cooking liquid and combine with 9 tbsp/125 g of the sugar. Add the cornstarch mixture to the berries and bring to a boil, stirring while the mixture thickens.

3 Stir in the cinnamon and cool the compote.

4 Beat the cream for about 3 minutes (it should still pour easily). Then gently blend in the remaining sugar and vanilla mark.

5 Spoon the Red Currant Compote into 4 dessert glasses and garnish with the beaten cream and reserved red currants. Serve with lady fingers.

Serves 4

1¼ lb/600 g red currants (ca. 4¾ cups)

3 tbsp cornstarch

⅔ cup/150 g sugar

½ tsp ground cinnamon

generous ¾ cup/200 ml heavy cream

mark from ½ vanilla bean

Prep. time: ca. 25 minutes (plus cooking time) Per portion ca. 375 kcal/1575 kJ 3 g P, 15 g F, 53 g C

159

Peaches in Honey
Honungsbakad persika

1 Blanch the peaches briefly in hot water. Then peel and halve them, and remove the stones.

2 Melt the honey in a saucepan over a low heat. Add the orange juice and about 3 tbsp water, and blend together.

3 Bring this mixture to a boil and simmer the peach halves in it for about 5 minutes.

4 Preheat the oven to 390 °F/200 °C. Remove the peaches from the saucepan and place in a greased baking dish, with the cut side facing up. Pour the honey syrup over the peaches.

5 Soften the butter and then combine with the sugar and ground nuts. Sprinkle the nut mixture over the peaches. Bake in the oven until golden brown, then trickle the liqueur over the peaches. Service with vanilla ice cream or vanilla sauce.

Serves 4

4 large peaches

4 tbsp honey

freshly squeezed juice of 2 oranges

3½ tbsp/50 g butter plus extra for the dish

4 tbsp brown sugar

4 tbsp ground nuts

4 tsp apricot liqueur

Prep. time: ca. 20 minutes (plus baking time) Per portion ca. 195 kcal/817 kJ 2 g P, 8 g F, 27 g C

Recipe Index